THE WELL

THE ART OF DRAWING OUT AUTHENTIC CONVERSATIONS

ENDORSEMENTS

In her book, *The Well, The Art of Drawing Out Authentic Conversations*, author Cathy Krafve touches on an important point. How do we take conversations to the next level? This book contains some excellent communication ideas to enhance and improve all our relationships.
—**Josh D. McDowell**, author

A key part of my day job is training counselors to help hurting people by 'drawing out' what's at the heart of a conflict—to help them face and actually have those key conversations that can turn into healthy communication. Every once in a while, a book like *The Well* comes along that becomes 'required reading' for them to do just that. Cathy's transparency, honesty, biblical wisdom, and pages of helpful, practical tools can help you quit putting off—and actually have—those 'We need to talk' conversations. This is a 'must read' now.
—**John Trent**, PhD, President, StrongFamilies.com, author of *LifeMapping* and co-author of *The Blessing*

Cathy Krafve has written a significant book on the art of effective communication that will be an important read for businesspeople, educators, spouses, and others. As a professional communicator, I highly recommend *The Well, The Art of Drawing Out Authentic Conversations* to all who desire to be more effective in their conversations with others.
—**Janet Holm McHenry**, national speaker and author of twenty-four books, including the bestselling *PrayerWalk: Becoming a Woman of Prayer, Strength, and Discipline*

The Well, The Art of Drawing Out Authentic Conversations is like a cup of cold water to wake up our halfhearted conversations. The author offers readers refreshing conversation, insights, tips, and techniques sure to give them greater impact and influence."
—**Lori Boruff**, speaker, writer, and Christian Communicators co-director

That you are a person of influence is a given. Whether it's negative or positive is determined in no small part by the effectiveness of your communication skills. In *The Well, The Art of Drawing Out Authentic Conversations*, Cathy Krafve rightly identifies communication as the catalyst to intimate and substantive relationships.

—**Bobby C. Dagnel**, Senior Pastor, First Baptist Church, Lubbock, Texas

Cathy *can* talk tough, not like John Wayne, but in the gentlest, most compassionate way. She has a way of wrapping her words around your heart because she is as transparent as Saran Wrap. *The Well* explains how to live life the best way possible—through learning the gift of good communication.

—**Tammy Whitehurst**, professional speaker and co-owner of the Christian Communicators Conference

I wish everybody could meet Cathy. She's vivacious in her words and in her voice. But also, you never walk away discouraged when you talk with Cathy.

—**Pastor James Dill**, founder of Shepherd's Heart, Tyler, Texas

Cathy Krafve's new book, *The Well*, is a guide on how to communicate effectively, especially when the conversation is a hard one. Cathy shares learned techniques on how to have that win-win conversation.

—**Charlotte Canion**, award-winning author of *You Have to Laugh to Keep from Crying: How to Parent Your Parents*

Cathy Krafve is a woman who loves a good quote, Jesus, and her family. Like a good general, Cathy maps out battle-worthy strategies for everyday situations in her latest book, *The Well, The Art of Drawing Out Authentic Conversation*. She tells you all about entrenched defenses and how to deploy 'Conversational Adventures,' without actually starting World War III.

—**Frankie Picasso**, CEO of The Good Radio Network and four-time bestselling author.

THE WELL

THE ART OF DRAWING OUT AUTHENTIC CONVERSATIONS

CATHY PRIMER KRAFVE

PUBLISHING THE POSITIVE
ELK LAKE PUBLISHING INC.
Plymouth, Massachusetts

Cover and Interior Design: Derinda Babcock

Editor(s): Sue Fairchild, Susan K. Stewart, Deb Haggerty

Author Represented by: Karen Neumair, Credo Communications LLC

PUBLISHED BY: Elk Lake Publishing, Inc., 35 Dogwood Drive, Plymouth, MA 02360, 2020

Library Cataloging Data

Names: Krafve, Cathy Primer (Cathy Primer Krafve)

The Well: The Art of Drawing Out Authentic Conversation / Cathy Primer Krafve

222 p. 23cm × 15cm (9in × 6 in.)

Identifiers: ISBN-13: 978-1-951970-29-1 (paperback) | 978-1-951970-30-7 (trade paperback) | 978-1-951970-31-4 (e-book)

Key Words: Modern family, community, difficult conversations, crucial conversations, Jesus, Christian books, Family communication cohesion, communication in marriage.

LCCN: 2020934891 Nonfiction

DEDICATION

This book is dedicated to three influential people, our children: Anna Krafve Pierce, Ellen Krafve Trant, and William Krafve. As your dad always says, "You kids are a bright spot of light wherever you are in the world."

And this book is also dedicated to our Fireside Tribe of fellowship-loving friends. What would we do without your input, wisdom, stories, prayers, and encouragement? We thank God in every remembrance of you.

TABLE OF CONTENTS

ACKNOWLEDGMENTS

I Am Grateful

I am thankful for all the encouragement I've received to write, especially from my family. We believe a single message impacts a culture—multiple voices mean even more blessing.

To Sandra Beck, who continues to inspire me with her unfailing love and support, not to mention her genius at all things media and message, thank you. My best hope is to honor your faith in me by honoring God, since there's no way I can repay all the kindness you've bestowed on me throughout the creative process and in life.

Without the subtle and succinct Christi McGuire, my personal editor and friend, this book would still comprise one big muddle. Christi, you amaze me in a concise, well-edited way. Thank you for being yourself in all the best ways as a friend who encourages and builds fellowship.

Thank you to our friends and "partners in the positive" at Elk Lake Publishing. First, to Susan Stewart for believing in the potential of our Camp Krafve projects. Then, to Deb Haggerty for leading the way in creating community and family out of a bunch of innovative, creative, independent types. Thank you to Sue Fairchild for walking me through the editing process with grace, patience, respect, and oh-so-much expertise. Sue, your fingerprints are all over this one. Plus, I am grateful to Derinda Babcock for her amazing ability to transform ideas into covers worth their weight in words.

Thank you to the many women and men, heroes and friends all, who courageously share their stories and wisdom on *Fireside Talk Radio*. Because of you, our world is a better place. Also, thank you to my favorite co-hosts, Anna Krafve Pierce and Ellen Krafve Trant.

Additionally, thanks to the friends whom I met through the Mount Hermon Christian Writers Conference where publishing experts showed up every spring to help the rest of us.

One thing leads to another. At Mount Hermon, I met Credo Communication's Karen Neumair. I immediately recognized her talent, like Jesus, for focusing on individuals while establishing extensive relationships. After much begging, pleading, fingernail biting, oh, and prayer too, she agreed to represent me. In our first hour of conversation, she answered questions I had carried around for years.

Additionally, I'm thankful for those Bible scholars, writers, and pastors, whose encouragement in my spiritual journey means more than I can say. I am particularly grateful for any corrective perspectives they so generously shared for this book when asked, not to mention some quotable history lessons. They include Bobby Dagnel, James Dill, David Dykes, Chris Legg, Ben A. Simpson, Ross Strader, and, for this book, two of our own pastors at Galilee Baptist, Randy Ector and Anthony Williams.

Thank you to my mighty praying friends, particularly Susan Ellsworth, Grace English, Sandra Ford, Dawn Franks, Sandra Merville Hart, Cynthia Howland, Frances Keaton, Darlene Marshall, Janet McHenry, Mary Ottman, Helen Robinson, Laurie Rossman, Angie Ruark, Gail Scott, Deb Smith, Eugenia Key Son, Grace Steele, Rayla Styles, and Pam Van Meter, to name just a few treasured praying women. Plus, there are my esteemed lunch bunch prayer warriors: Bess Arnold, Darla Bennett, Bobbie Dance, Sandy King, Cathy Powell, and Diane Thomason. Additionally, author, friend, and Mount Hermon roommate Kathryn Spurgeon who prayerfully read my proposal and offered invaluable insight. Thank you for praying, dear friends. I'm convinced this would not have happened without your prayers.

To friends with newspaper experience, like Jay Graham, Amy Pearson, Chad Wilson, Don Truel, and Betty Jones, thank you for your camaraderie. I especially want to thank Bill and

Jessica Woodall, of Bluebonnet Publishing, who allowed me to write my weekly column in the *Bullard Banner*, one of my favorite newspapers in all the world, and believe me, I am a connoisseur of newspapers.

Also, my friends at Christian Communicators, Tammy Whitehurst and Lori Boruff, with a shout out to Sherry Poundstone and the Class of 2018, who helped prepare me for the road ahead and connected me to a whole network of folks committed to spreading transformative messages.

Along with our children, this book is dedicated to our invaluable Camp Krafve Fireside Tribe. You provide wise interactions, thoughtful questioning, accountability, and inspire me to draw deeper from the place in my soul where I long to give you the best. To the many conversationally adventurous listening, reading, and praying friends who join us in desiring to share positive, enriching messages in our culture, it is my privilege to join with you.

Beyond all else, I am thankful for my family where I learned from an early age this powerful truth—communication is essential for companionship. To our siblings, cousins, and their families, thank you for continuing the tradition of hanging in there to foster togetherness into two more generations.

Best of all, thank you, David, for committing to conversational adventure when communication seems impossible and painful. My best joy is to courageously share life with you, my beloved David.

Finally, to the One who is worthy of praise, to God be the glory.

> Now to Him who is able to do exceedingly abundantly above all that we ask or think, according to the power that works in us, to Him be glory in the church by Christ Jesus to all generations, forever and ever. Amen. (Ephesians 3:20–21)

INTRODUCTION

WHY BOTHER?

Initiating the authentic conversations we most desire takes guts. How do you convince your spouse it's time for change? Can you persuade a teenager to listen when you warn them again about bad influences? Do you wish your aging parent would let you help? What about telling your family you had an abortion more than forty years ago? If those seem like specific examples, it's because I've had all those conversations.

In each of the above examples—and thousands of others every day—we must step up with courage to create the authentic conversations we crave.

In a lighthearted example, an exasperated mother may admonish her adorable toddler not to play with Mommy's scissors. Even though the child says, "Yes, Mommy," the next thing you know, the little one is trying the scissors out on the new sofa anyway. Okay, maybe that did happen at my house. Do you have those days, too?

The only thing lost is a pillow on the couch, but what about when the toddler grows into a teen and the consequences become much more complicated?

I groan to think of all the years I wasted on communication strategies that didn't work. We all want to be heard and respected when it really matters, not just when the sofa pillows are at stake. Some folks seem to get their messages across better than others. Are those people naturally influential? What qualifies them to create authentic conversations while others seem unqualified? What can disqualify me?

If you're wondering why I wrote this book, that's easy. Being unheard wore me out. I desired authentic conversations with those I love and wondered if there were better ways to express my ideas. Could I achieve breakthroughs in communication with my own family?

No more sweeping things under the rug. No more pretending or avoiding controversial topics. I wanted to share the most sacred, important parts of our lives—sacred stories of mercy and forgiveness. Did I have the courage for the tough conversations required to transform relationships?

The answer was yes. And at our house, we learned to call those transformative discussions conversational adventures.

WHAT ARE CONVERSATIONAL ADVENTURES?

Our family uses the phrase "conversational adventures" to define "difficult but crucial conversations." Truth can be scary. Tough topics call for courageous hearts. By using the word "adventure," we open ourselves up to the idea of taking a risk. Managed risk often produces miraculous and inspiring results—sort of like hiking a steep trail requires courage but affords terrific views.

"We need to talk." Have you ever been caught off guard by this phrase, especially by a boss or, worse, your child's principal? We all know the dreadful feeling. The conversation is off to a bad start and hasn't even started yet.

"At the heart of almost all chronic problems in our organizations, our teams, our relationships lie crucial conversations—ones we're either not holding or not holding well. Twenty years of research involving more than 100,000 people reveals the key skill of effective leaders, teammates, parents, and loved ones is the capacity to skillfully address emotionally and politically risky issues."[1]

Gentle truth unites and inspires us all when delivered with grace and skill. In Texas, on a blistering hot day, nothing is more refreshing than an icy glass of tangy lemonade. After an authentic conversation, filled with compassion and mutual understanding, two friends can hug each other tenderly, deeply refreshed.

Unlike drinking fresh lemonade, however, there are risks involved when it comes to telling the truth. What strategies can we use to produce the authentic conversations we pursue? In the coming pages, you will discover more than forty different ways to enhance your communication skill set. You'll see exactly which strategies Jesus used to draw out an authentic conversation with the woman at the well.

AUTHENTIC CONVERSATIONS

Like me, you may desire authentic conversations. Maybe you, too, have sacred—highly valued and personal—stories you want to share with those you love. However, sometimes we fear the response of others when we seek to share our most personal stories. Perhaps we fear condemnation or rejection.

Nearly all people fear rejection. We're tired of discussions morphing into arguments. I totally get it. In these pages, I will joyfully share communication strategies gleaned from the master communicator, Jesus himself.

I don't know about you, but my world gets messy in a hurry. A stubborn toddler puts her hands on her hips and stamps her foot, and suddenly, I'm wondering why I feel compelled to enforce weird rules from my childhood. A client unintentionally punches one of my emotional triggers, and I'm sorely tempted to lose my temper. I say one grumpy thing to my hubby after a long day, and now, no one understands me. *Sniff, sniff.*

Even worse than my little inner dramas, though, are the real pain and suffering folks are experiencing in our culture. This world needs miracles.

Influencing our world for pure good seems essential, especially when we factor in the suffering all around us. But how does one ever feel qualified for such a breathtaking assignment?

If you're familiar with standard Bible studies, this look at Scripture may surprise you. We'll approach specific verses looking for any and all aspects of conversational adventure. Together, we'll target the communication strategies Jesus used with the woman at the well. As expert communicators, we'll claim better tools to share with each other.

If these two thoughts permeate every page of this book, then I've done my job:

1. Communication is the pathway to companionship.
2. Jesus is the great communicator.

Jesus is described in many ways. In the Book of John, Jesus is described as the λογοσ or logos (John 1:1–17). Logos is translated literally as "word." The Word created the world and all that's in it. The Word was born of woman and died to save us. The Word communicated truth to us through his life. We, therefore, should pay attention to the way Jesus communicated.

As we watch for the communication tools and strategies Jesus chose, we learn from the master communicator how to manage the most complex conversational adventures.

I really love the way the disciples share their joyful experience of recognizing Jesus as God himself.

> That which was from the beginning, which we have heard, which we have seen with our eyes, which we have looked upon, and our hands have handled, concerning the Word of life—the life was manifested, and we have seen, and bear witness, and declare to you that eternal life which was with the Father and was manifested to us—that which we have seen and heard we declare to you, that you also may have fellowship with us; and truly our fellowship *is* with the Father and with His Son Jesus Christ. And these things we write to you that your joy may be full." (I John 1:1–4)

The disciples wanted us to know Jesus as they did, the one who was "from the beginning." Can't you just feel the jubilation they feel as they invite us to know him, too?

God became incarnate (came to earth in the flesh as a baby) to speak directly to humanity. Obviously, God speaks to us in the beauty all around us. In all he created, God reveals his goodness. Yet, there is something miraculous in the way the Holy Spirit announces to Mary that her Son will be the long-awaited Savior (Matthew1:18–21, Like 1:28–33). I think incarnation is a strong concept for a book about conversations. Jesus's life is his message to us.

As we watch for the communication tools and strategies Jesus chose, we learn from the master communicator how to manage the most complex conversational adventures. As a result, pure influence, integrity, and joy ripple out in our lives. Spirit and truth can permeate our conversations as we practice patience and compassion. We can enjoy the benefit of joining others in influencing our world for good in our families, our churches, and our communities.

FROM SOLITARY FIGURE TO COMMUNITY INFLUENCER

As women, we can relate whenever anyone describes the woman at the well's experience. You may have heard this story taught with her as the central figure. Perhaps you heard she's the woman none of the other women would talk to.

They say she was once pretty. Okay, let's face it—she's still downright beautiful, if you like that kind of superficial glamor. Probably won't get invited to the next wedding or baby shower at the church, though. She's not our cup of tea. She won't look the other women in the eyes either, because, well, everybody knows what she's been up to and with whom. In fact, we rarely see her out during the daytime because she likes one-on-one companionship, if you know what that means (wink, wink).

As we study the story, we realize this woman was transformed from a solitary figure to a woman of influence in her community. Instead of seeing her as lonely and pitiful, what if we described her as tenacious and courageous? In fact, her testimony still impacts lives today, thousands of years later. What a contribution this lady made to her community!

THE WELL

Maybe we should look at this old story in a new light. In fact, let's adopt her right now as our personal friend and soul sister.

Finally, before we're finished, we'll gain a deep and abiding conviction of our own worthiness and calling to be people of influence. We don't always realize our painful experiences or most cherished memories can be used by God. God transforms our worst hurts into sacred stories when we turn them over to him for his glory and purpose. In fact, if you have any doubt God intends for you to influence all the lives of those around you, including those culprits in your own family who are most likely to tune you out, hold on to your hat. We are about to take the ride of our lives into the territory of pure influence. And what a wild ride it is. Giddyap!

CHAPTER 1:
THE COMMUNICATION CHALLENGE

HOW CAN I EXTEND MY INFLUENCE?

ONE RELATIONSHIP AT A TIME, STARTING WITH SPIRIT AND TRUTH.

> God is Spirit, and those who worship Him must worship in spirit and truth. (John 4:24)

How many hours had we been fighting? Had it been days? We were past the honeymoon stage, that was for sure. With two toddlers at home, I needed shoring up. I begged, pleaded, demanded emotional support from my husband, but David was all out of energy too. I stared at the man I loved and silently considered my options.

"I'm sick and tired of your feelings," he said.

In a rare fit of authenticity, I surprised him with my response.

"I'm sick of my feelings too!"

Thus began my long quest to understand the best way to communicate when conversation becomes near impossible. I wanted spirit and truth, mixed with compassion, to be the hallmarks of conversations in my home. And not just at home, but in my workplace and community too.

During another difficult conversation, I blinked as I silently processed what the boss had told me. *Oh, brother, that's stress sweat dripping under my arms. Should I try to reason with him? If I present my idea again, will my coworkers assume I'm arguing with the boss? Worse, will he think I'm intentionally undermining his authority? Of course, I have to let it go. Again.*

I still find communication challenging even with a degree in the subject, a lifetime of practice, and a business based on messaging. In fact, it's so hard, I sometimes find myself wondering *Why even bother to communicate?*

The answer is simple. Better communication matters because conversation forms the basis of all healthy human relationships.

In his book, *Everyone Communicates, Few Connect*, John Maxwell states, "Any message you try to convey must contain a piece of you."[2] Gentle truth, spiced with patience and compassion, helps us connect with others.

Jesus, the master communicator, understood the connectivity of truth, compassion, and patience. In his conversation with the woman at the well (recorded in John 4), Jesus demonstrated more than forty principles for us to explore today. In addition, he seasoned all his conversations, including this one, with his Spirit and truth. Sharing our most personal self—being truthful—is the key to connecting. That means drawing into the deeply spiritual places of our hearts.

You may wonder if you even have what it takes to be influential. There is only one characteristic required for influence: *readiness*. If you are ready, you are pre-qualified. God designed you to be a person of influence.

In this first chapter on extending our personal influence one relationship at a time, we'll look at five things:

- How is conversational adventure a relationship enhancer?
- What is the goal of every conversation?
- What are the roadblocks and risks?
- How can we manage the risks of conversational adventure?
- What can we learn from Jesus's conversation with the woman at the well?

Conversational Adventure: A Relationship Enhancer

Spoiler alert. I hate to tell the end of the story at the beginning of a book, but perhaps you already know the story of the woman at the well and her influence.

As her story unfolds in John 4, the Bible tells us the woman came to the well alone. Jesus began a conversation by asking her for water. They engaged in an authentic conversational adventure. Then, she rushed to share the story of her encounter with the Savior with others. What a sacred moment in the life of a community.

What does it look like when we decide to risk a conversational adventure? Perhaps we broach a topic everyone else in the office is hoping will magically disappear. Maybe we risk having an argument with a spouse because the situation is serious. We decide to talk tough to our teenagers, as we pray they won't turn down the wrong path. You've shared a secret, and then held your breath to see if your best friend would reject you. You've already embarked on a conversational adventure.

Why call it an adventure instead of simply a tough conversation? First, like any adventure, the risks associated with difficult conversations add an element of danger and require courage. Second, in most cases, we prepare for difficult conversations meticulously and analyze all potential mishaps beforehand, much like we would prepare for a hike or an afternoon at the lake. Third, the outcome may surprise us— even bring about exciting change. Finally, difficult discussions may feel more like a verbal expedition, rather than one simple conversation. They may involve endurance.

One conversation may not do the trick. The process of communication often entails a series of challenging conversations. Yet, ongoing conversation is the key to long-term companionship. Companionship can only be real in our lives if we put aside feelings of rejection and embrace people where we all live in our own humanness. Baring our souls and being authentic requires courage.

These types of conversational adventures enhance all our relationships. We become more vulnerable. We connect on a deeper level with others. We can share those things that make our hearts heavy, and in return, we let others share theirs. For instance, when I share with my editor that writing makes me tremble, she immediately encourages me, and our relationship is strengthened.

In another example, I hate to admit how unaware I was of the trauma men suffer in our culture. On several occasions, men have shared with me how they have become victims of violence. Brutality is hard to comprehend and even harder to talk about. Because of those courageous individuals who shared their story with me, I better understand the pain many men carry around in silence.

Not only that, but my respect and empathy for each of those gentlemen grew beyond measure. Our conversations enhanced our own relationships. Plus, their willingness to talk about difficult experiences helped me understand the pressures men face in general, thus enhancing all my future relationships.

As we consider the silent suffering all around us, we begin to understand what Jesus meant when he pointed out the direct connection between spirit and truth, especially when it comes to worshiping God. To truly worship God fully, our wounded spirits must seek healing. We must delve deeply into the truth hidden in our own souls.

How can we build meaningful relationships with others when so much of our pain is hidden? We must let go of our pretenses and learn to speak truthfully about our own deepest fears and frailties to nurture deep, authentic companionship. When we share our weakest places with trustworthy friends, mutual empathy blossoms, as many good men and women have proven to me.

Additionally, learning to lean on the confidential wisdom of deeply authentic friends enhances all our relationships in a ripple effect. We grow in confidence and can then offer our understanding and compassion to others. Learning to be authentic with even one trustworthy friend enhances all our other relationships. We become more likely to dwell in gentle companionship with everyone God brings across our path.

THE GOAL OF EVERY CONVERSATIONAL ADVENTURE

The goal of every conversational adventure is to inspire deeper understanding, a form of spiritual connection sometimes called fellowship. Communication is the basis of all companionship, and good communication skills are the prerequisite for good relationships. Naturally, conversation is a complex mix of listening, talking, and being heard.

We all desire to be heard, of course. But there's a big difference between listening and being heard. Shelves of books are written on the topic of proactive listening, body language, storytelling, and countless other topics associated with communicating.

Most of us prefer to interact with people who will listen, understand, and respect our perspectives. Communication involves mutual respect.

However, the goal of mutual respect often eludes us. We want the information we offer to sink in and to make a difference to the other person. Of course, we also need to hear the other person and to let their words sink into our hearts.

In a world saturated with social media, it's easy to assume communication is shouting out a message. Communication is not speaking *at* one another, though. Communication, like conversation, should be a two-way street. Deep conversations result when we listen and hear one another, sharing honestly. I like the word *ponder* for describing the process of considering different perspectives and thus growing in our mutual understanding and respect.

Influence, at its best, is a mutual process. We all want to be heard, not just listened to momentarily. Some people call this "being seen." We want to see, to hear, and to respect others for who they are just as we want to be treated the same way. Authentic conversations allow us to cultivate mutual understand and respect.

The goal of conversational adventure is to inspire deeper understanding. Hearing requires pondering and imagination to understand the other person's perspective. Tough topics often require prayerful attention to digest all perspectives with compassion. Take an example from the life of a preteen and her mom.

She walked to school at the crack of dawn, bundled up in her soft jacket, her face flush with embarrassment. She leaned forward and pulled her hoodie closer around her head. Cars zipped past her, and parents who loved their kids dropped them off at school.

"Mom, I don't want to walk to school anymore," she exclaimed after school as she slammed her books on the kitchen table.

"Why not, honey?"

"I don't know why! It's just embarrassing," replied the preteen child. Her heart knew more but was afraid to speak. *If Mom loved me, wouldn't she drive me to school like the other kids?*

A few days later, the preteen heard a honk in the driveway. Mom had arranged for a neighbor to pick up her daughter each morning. Mom thought *Problem solved.* Daughter thought *It still feels like she doesn't love me.*

The mom in this story assumed she knew how to fix the problem based on what her daughter said. Because the daughter didn't truly express her inner thoughts, the deep need for connection didn't get met. Mom should have, perhaps, asked insightful questions to dig deeper for the information she needed from her daughter about her feelings. But sometimes even good questions don't draw out enough information for us to understand the other person's perspective.

Maybe the mom here didn't want an argument as so often happened when communicating with her daughter. Conversations involve taking turns listening and speaking. Many times, we may need to pray and ponder before we ever utter a word. Like the mom in the story, we may try to find creative solutions to problems we really don't understand.

There are also times when the wealth of information shared may overwhelm us. After we've talked and shared with someone, we may need to ponder what was said. The goal is to understand and respect each other's viewpoints. We may need to pray to regain our patience. Perhaps we need God's help, so we don't take things too personally.

Some conversations truly challenge our last drop of fortitude. Our souls may feel dehydrated as if we've worked all day in the blazing sunlight with no relief.

With conversational adventures, our true goal is to expand our influence for pure good. Influence increases even when people disagree with us, because they trust our willingness to be vulnerable. Some people use the word *authentic*. There are no pretensions when being authentic. Soon, because of our vulnerability, fellowship permeates all our relationships.

ROADBLOCKS TO COMMUNICATION

The journey of creating authentic conversations is not for wimps. We all face roadblocks when we try to engage in effective communication. Every family has someone who fails to respect our perspective.

For example, there's always that one guest who insists on asking to bring her darling Doberman with territorial issues into your home, no matter how often you've explained your dogs will be traumatized by hers. After a few suggestions about alternative plans for her pet, you may have to put down firm boundaries.

Maybe the challenging person is not a guest, but someone you live with and love very much. Perhaps they dismiss your opinions or fears without hearing why your concerns seem logical and justified to you. Maybe your boss is easily threatened by new ideas or strong personalities.

What if someone you care about hits a snag and you really, I mean *really*, need them to hear you? "I spoke. He listened, but he didn't hear," commented a close friend. We've all been there. Whether it's with a boss, coworker, spouse, one of our kids, or an aging parent, some conversations are just plain tough.

On the one hand, we don't expect to agree with everyone, even those we love. On the other hand, it would be nice if we don't feel singed every time we broach a delicate topic. Knowing where to begin and how to have difficult conversations can be complicated. Nowhere is that truer than in our own families. Consider another example I experienced many years ago.

"Do you always talk to each other like that?" asked my friend in a hushed whisper after David left.

I felt my face turn red. *What would she think if she saw us fully engaged in an argument?*

"I hate to admit, we tend to get really intense," I answered, cringing.

"No, what I meant was, you talked it through in front of me and didn't leave angry."

Relief flooded my soul. My husband and I had learned to work out certain topics without hitting a wall and becoming angry. *We are making progress.* Even after all these years, however, family conversations can still be tricky at our house. My hubby and offspring tend to be every bit as strong and intense as I am.

The latest technologies—cell phones, tablets, video games—become roadblocks too. How can we expect to be heard when our attentions are fixed to a screen? Especially at home, our hearts yearn for companionship and connection. We long to turn off our devices and tune in to our families.

We all know how to talk, but communicating can get tense. Perhaps, like me, you've added writing, blogging, podcasting, you name it, to find ways to communicate. I'll try almost anything to connect. Even after years of studying what works, I still find myself frustrated, and I'm supposed to be a communications expert.

THE RISKS

There are risky things we can't possibly know when we try to have deep conversations. Other people don't, and often can't, share their hearts. Therefore, we're tempted to draw false conclusions about their motives. Such challenges frustrate us, testing our patience and sending us false and risky signals.

Here's a silly example of how private distress can give a false impression. I'm normally outgoing and talkative. While on vacation in Cabo, however, I spent an afternoon on a tour alone without meeting a single new person. How could this be? Simple. I forgot to go to the bathroom before I got on the boat. I was so focused on keeping my legs crossed, I never said a word to anyone. When the boat finally docked, I ran to the nearest restroom. If anyone noticed, they might have assumed I was a snob, or the mafia was after me.

Anyone can experience private distress that taps emotional stamina, and not just due to momentary potty-break emergencies. We can't possibly guess the private distress others may feel, so we must train ourselves to tune in to clues. This ability to tune in helps us develop compassion.

When we try to reach out in difficult conversations, we risk rejection. Others may be suffering from private distress. When we make false assumptions—taking their distraction as personal rejection—we put relationships at risk. In contrast, compassion requires us to put our imagination to work in positive ways. Distress can come in many forms, often fitting into five categories: physical, emotional, spiritual, moral, or financial.

Private distress can slam into us in the form of a sudden diagnosis, like cancer. Ongoing physical distress can also sneak up on us in a slow, chronic deterioration of our health. For example, when a knee injury in a youthful basketball game leads to knee replacement surgery later in life, a person may be stretched thin by daily chronic pain for years. Anyone may tolerate unseen pain without the knowledge of coworkers, friends, or even family. Rather than avoiding conversations, our compassionate understanding is required.

Emotional pain may not manifest in an outward way. For example, in college, I tried to put my envy aside when a friend seemed to receive every honor imaginable at the University of Texas. We were sorority sisters, and I loved her to pieces, but give me a break. She was beautiful, smart, engaged to a big man on campus, and chosen for numerous awards. Then, to top it off, she was chosen as a finalist for the school's top honor. I should have relished the fact such an amazing woman counted me among her friends. Instead, I struggled with jealousy.

One day, there was a knock on my dorm door. She stood in my doorway asking to have a quiet conversation with me. Her mother was suffering serious chronic health issues, and she needed prayer. Suddenly, my personal battle with envy melted away. I felt truly blessed to be her friend. Oh, my fickle heart. We never know what may be happening beneath the surface in the lives of those we love.

Overwhelming grief can often short-circuit people's minds too. When my mom passed away, debilitating pain engulfed me, hindering my ability to process my thoughts and emotions for several months. In fact, I have no memories at all of the month after her death. Yet, surely, I interacted with other people—probably like a sleepwalker in an unseen fog.

Sometimes physical and emotional stress can conspire for a double whammy. A teenager may be marinating in hormones, turning inward emotionally. Toddlers can get unreasonable just because they need a nap. Don't we all get a little unreasonable when we need a nap?

In addition, spiritual and moral stressors often compound each other. A coworker may be struggling through a private hell, like a divorce or addiction. Moral decisions, even of others, may catastrophically impact our lives. We may find ourselves in spiritual crisis as we face life's challenges.

Then there's the financial distress we all experience, sometimes culture-wide, but often in private. Unexpected medical bills may throw off our game. A grown child gets into trouble, and parents may feel compelled to help financially. So many things can be brewing behind the scenes in people's lives.

Communication gets risky when we try to talk with someone who refuses to take personal responsibility for their own wrongdoing or faulty attitude. Perhaps you've been blamed just because you tried to talk.

We've all dodged responsibility for our actions at one time or other. Communication shuts down when someone is in denial, whether it's a spouse, a boss, a colleague, or, um, yes, even us. A person may go on the defensive.

Individuals often have their unique reasons for refusing to hear any perspective but their own. These can even be triggers from their childhood, which have no bearing on the present. Unseen circumstances can make conversational adventures especially risky. Danger ahead!

MANAGING THE RISK WITH EFFECTIVE STRATEGIES

As we will see, the woman at the well had legitimate questions and objections. Jesus responded respectfully to her, giving her opportunity to process his input. I think you will love his example of ignoring her objections initially to focus on her heart.

Jesus demonstrated tools and strategies to stretch and enhance *your communication skills*, whatever challenges and risks to communication exist in your life today. God's divine intention is for us to exercise our pure influence, no matter how messy our world seems. He designed us to engage with him and others in the most spiritual, authentic, and truthful way.

How can we expect to ever have effective conversations with so many roadblocks and risks? Fortunately, the conversational adventure between Jesus and the woman at the well provides us with lots of strategies. Once we decide the risk is worth the potential gain, good communication strategies maximize our chances of success.

What is worth fighting for in your life? Once you answer that question, you'll be ready for conversational adventure.

As we begin to think of tough conversations in a good way, as adventures, we can gain confidence. With better communication skills, we're able to create better, more enriching conversations. We begin to move in a healthy direction because our conversations reflect our love and respect for others. Our influence for God's kingdom is expanded as mutual understanding grows.

Like Jesus, we can focus on one person today. We can be confident God has a plan to extend our influence. Our goal is to help others reach their potential as we stretch to fulfill our own God-given potential. We may even change the community to boot.

As we learn to manage the risks, we push through to enjoy the trek just as hikers take on the adventure of a difficult trail. We don't give up halfway before we reach the summit. We commit to the process of loving each other by staying with the conversation to the end. The thrills include deeper understanding, mutual respect, and sweeter companionship.

THE WELL

WHAT WE LEARN FROM JESUS

To live authentic lives, we must be bold yet gentle as we address difficult topics. Living fiercely eternal, yet gently present lives takes courage and patience. We want to build trust and mutual respect in all our relationships. We see this very approach in Jesus's own earthly life and conversations. Although gently present, he focused on eternity with intensity. This type of life takes an adventurer's heart.

Of course, conversations don't always work out the way we wish they would. Still, there is glory in the adventure. Like the view from the top of the mountain, sometimes we must climb through some rough terrain to get there.

With a deep breath and a lot of courage, we decide to move into uncharted territory. Truth is so important, it requires we step out and take risks. If we want to be influential in our relationships, we do this with a spirit of love. In the coming chapters, we'll see how spirit and truth are inseparable. Jesus links them clearly in the ideas he shares with the woman at the well.

Spirit and truth remind me of mashed potatoes and gravy on Southern menus. We're so spoiled in Texas. We wouldn't think of having one without the other with our chicken fried steak. Like our favorite food combos, our instinctive love of spirit and truth together probably explains why we find authenticity so appealing.

Now when David and I hit on a tough topic, my heart swells with thanksgiving.

"Can you believe we figured that out without arguing," he often says. "Are you sure you're not mad at me?"

"No way! I agree with the decision." Unlike the young hubby who was sick of my feelings, David is the easiest person in my life to communicate with now. I hope it won't take you years to figure out the best ways to communicate.

The principles Jesus shares about spirit and truth become more beautiful and complex as we grow in our understanding of them.

Our goal is to empower ourselves to have conversational adventures, regardless of the other person. We don't control the response of the other person. Instead, we want to prepare to handle objections and stay authentic ourselves. We need to manage the risks and avoid the roadblocks to be powerful, effective communicators. Let's get started.

BEST QUESTION ABOUT INFLUENCE

What's standing in your way to expand the influence God intends for you to have?

Perhaps you're stymied by a simple thought: I am not qualified for influence. I'd like to help you change that mindset.

Americans take a lot for granted when it comes to communication. Probably because we are spoiled by the blessing of free speech. We seem to think speech should come naturally, freely, because of this term. But let's think about communication a different way. Most of us take two to three years to learn to talk and five to six years to read or write. Childhood is finished before we can formulate abstract concepts into short thesis papers.

Why feel defeated because of an ongoing challenge to be heard? Why not give yourself years, literally years, to acquire new communication skills? Perhaps that reduces some of the pressure. Once you free yourself from the pressure of communicating quickly, set a short-term goal. Use this book to acquire some new skills. You can do so by taking a minute at the end of each chapter to reflect.

The woman at the well turned the course of history for an entire community of people. All it took was a readiness to interact and a willingness to listen to the Savior. To me this is one of the transforming truths from the passage. We know her testimony drew others to the Savior. What would we add to the simple truth that she opened herself up in a conversation with Jesus?

Why not accept this truth today? He meant for us to be heard and respected. You might as well face the fact and get on with owning the influence God intends for you. You, too, can turn the course of history for the community of people you love and influence.

It is not vainglorious to pursue influence, even though it may seem the opposite of humility. We're living in such a messy world it's okay to claim our influence, if we do so in a kind and compassionate way.

Our devotion to those we love compels us to influence them for pure good. Practicing better communication skills allows us to create authentic conversations. Leaders who master the art of authentic conversation extend their influence by engaging others.

Perhaps we train a child to slow down and focus on their homework. Maybe a teenager needs input about decisions. Young adults may struggle to process all the competing philosophies in the world today. Authentic conversations allow us to listen and gain the understanding we need. Then, we can offer encouragement and wisdom, thus influencing others in positive ways in a thousand small daily examples.

Our culture is "going to seed," as they say out here in the country where I live. The weeds are overtaking pasture in our culture. There's not a moment to lose. Even if we start small, we'd better use our influence any way we can today. Each authentic conversation we initiate becomes a chance to spread better understanding and compassion all around. Who knows what the generations after us could do with the communication skills we acquire and pass on to them?

PRACTICAL TIP: ANSWER ONE QUESTION

Ask yourself one question: If you could use your influence in your family to accomplish something good and mighty, what would it be?

Make a short list of one or two ways your influence is needed in your home, at work, in your church, or in your community. After you've written down this list, give it to God in a simple prayer that expresses trust in him. You could even seal your list in an envelope and date it for two years from today. Then, start praying and watching for ways he may want to use you in that area. You may never look at your note again, but if you wait two years and peek, don't be surprised if you are walking in pure influence in those very areas.

May We Pray Together?

Dear Father, we often feel invisible and alone, like the woman at the well. When we try to speak your truth, we face a plethora of roadblocks and encounter many risks. We wonder if we are worthy of your attention. Will you hear us if we pray? Today, we come to you. We ask you to reach us in the most insecure places of our hearts. Teach us to recognize that you are giving us your undivided attention. You love to fill us with your presence. We desire your Spirit and truth to be united in us. Your presence in our hearts is our most sacred relationship. We invite you in. For this companionship with you, we thank you. We ask you to teach us to walk in your pure influence in this messy world we inhabit for now. Bless us because that's your heart's desire. In Jesus's name. Amen.

"Life is either a great adventure or nothing." –Helen Keller

CHAPTER 2:
COMMUNICATION NINJA

IS THERE ANY HOPE OF COMMUNICATING WITH FOLKS WHO CAN'T
(OR WON'T) HEAR?

YES, LIKE JESUS, WE CAN USE TWO-PART STRATEGIC COMPASSION
TO RELATE TO OTHERS.

> Therefore, when the Lord knew that the Pharisees
> had heard that Jesus made and baptized more
> disciples than John (though Jesus Himself did
> not baptize, but His disciples), He left Judea and
> departed again to Galilee. But He needed to go
> through Samaria. (John 4:1–4)

Throw Tupperware? Scream? I pictured myself, like an
action figure ninja, cutting his feet out from under him with
one kick, then pouncing to poke my thumbs in his eyeballs.
Options zipped through my brain with creative vigor. Obviously,
I watch too much television. Lord, have mercy! How in the
world could I get my hubby to hear me?

I know some authors recommend regular couch time away
from the kids for couples to reconnect with each other. At one
point in our marriage, couch time best described the monthly
meeting on our psychologist's couch trying to piece together
an unraveling marriage. Our counselor suggested we quit
assuming and trying to read each other's minds.

Still, a cartoon drawing of us at that moment could have told our counselor all he needed to know. From opposite corners of the couch, our arms folded across our chests and our bodies positioned away from each other, our toes tapped out a beat that said, "Let's get this over with. Now."

Home isn't the only place we need to communicate. Conversations with bosses, employees, clients, our children's teachers, or, worse, the principal test our best communication skills. The frustration can become so intense we feel like throwing in the towel almost before we get going. What are we to do?

Let's start with strategic compassion as a tool for reaching those who fail to hear. We'll look at how Jesus demonstrated strategic compassion in two ways. Plus, we'll look at a big benefit we get by ...

- understanding the two parts of strategic compassion— withdrawal and engagement,
- withdrawing from those who need time to ponder,
- seeking out those who are ready, and
- resting in self-care.

Two Parts of Strategic Compassion: Withdrawal and Engagement

We see the two parts of Jesus's strategic compassion in the opening verses of his conversation with the woman at the well. First, he withdraws from those who are unwilling to hear what he has to say—in this case, the Pharisees. Second, he makes himself available and responsive to someone who is ready to hear his message—the woman at the well.

Space can give other people time to ponder the truths we share. Strategic withdrawal from some people allows us to engage others with more enthusiasm and effectiveness. Plus, we show compassion to ourselves when we rest from a stressful situation.

Jesus was a gifted teacher of increasing notoriety and influence. Everywhere Jesus went, crowds flocked to him, demonstrating their responsiveness to the truth he taught.

In fact, Jesus attracted such a tribe—as we like to say in social media today—the powers-that-be (the Pharisees) started to take notice. Their attention was not necessarily a good thing.

John 4:6 tells us he was weary from his journey by the time he reached Sychar. Maybe he was also weary of fending off the Pharisees or keeping one step ahead of them. Perhaps Jesus withdrew from the Pharisees to give them time to ponder his message.

Although he could have simply withdrawn and rested away from all the crowds, he remained prepared to teach. Was he aware of this specific woman who seemed ready to hear him? Perhaps this is the reason he "needed" to go through Samaria. Like Jesus, we can also train ourselves to be alert to others' readiness as we withdraw to rest.

In doing these things, Jesus demonstrated a wonderful communication strategy for us—strategic compassion.

Jesus chose how to express his love for both the Pharisees and the woman at the well at the same time by using two different compassionate strategies. For the Pharisees, he withdrew and allowed them time to ponder his message. With the woman at the well, he chose to keep teaching because she was ready and waiting to hear his truth. I suspect her responsiveness even refreshed Jesus's soul—enhancing our third element of this mix, rest.

STRATEGIC COMPASSION RIPPLES OUT EVEN TODAY

How can utilizing strategic compassion create a ripple effect throughout a community in modern times? When I interviewed author and educator Ben Sciacca for *Fireside Talk Radio*, he told me how a respected mentor, Dr. Anthony Gordon, devoted himself to creating opportunities for kids in Birmingham, Alabama.

Dr. Gordon and his wife, Sharon, started *Restoration Academy in 1988 in response* to educational injustice in their community. They wanted to provide high-quality, private education to kids from families normally unable to afford such advantages.

It's tempting to accept the status quo and avoid the difficult conversations necessary whenever injustice is exposed. So often, injustice and self-righteousness dwell together. Today, like the Pharisees of Jesus's day, people may choose to believe change is impossible. Change can be considered counter cultural.

According to the Restoration Academy's mission statement, they "founded the school in response to divisive forces such as crime and violence that had ensnared many of the young people at his church and in his community."[1]

Ben labels those willing to take a risk for justice and peace, like Dr. and Mrs. Gordon, as "solutionaries." The responsibilities of everyday life and pastoring a church could have distracted Dr. Gordon from his dream of educational justice. Instead, the Gordons embarked on a conversational adventure with their community. Dr. Gordon, and the visionaries who joined him, set aside cultural distractions by using strategic compassion.

First, they invited everyone into an ongoing conversation, but they had to disregard naysayers as they focused on the vision of educational justice. Hence, they focused on those ready to listen. This represents the best form of strategic compassion in today's world. We must listen when others raise objections, but we don't have to succumb to those who say our dreams are impossible. We can withdraw from those who stand opposed to what God wants us to accomplish.

Instead of focusing on trying to change the minds of those unready to hear, we can work peacefully together with those who are ready to use their influence for good. Birmingham's Restoration Academy stands as a testimony to the power of vision and strategic compassion.

STRATEGIC COMPASSION IN WITHDRAWAL

There are no guarantees any other person will ever respect our views. Modern-day readers might wonder why Jesus chose to disengage from the Pharisees, thereby avoiding confrontation. This may seem counterintuitive. Sometimes, however, for us to be heard, the right strategy involves withdrawing to pray as we give others time to ponder. We all need time to think and rest.

Retreating can be a winning strategy and the most compassionate choice for all parties involved.

Retreat is a beautiful word, full of nuanced meaning. Instead of thinking of retreat as a withdrawal in defeat, as if we passively wimped out to avoid conflict, we can count refreshing retreats among our tools for strategic compassion.

The word retreat can mean a sabbatical, chosen for reflection, a withdrawal from normal routine to meet with the Lord. For example, think about women's retreats when churches carve out time away from our normal activities to focus on God.

When Jesus retreated to Samaria, a problem prompted him to withdraw. Too much attention for his teaching had sparked the ire of the Pharisees. Jesus's message was so powerful he attracted unwelcome attention.

Let's look at his response to the problem of too much attention, which developed due to his amazing ability to communicate effectively. In the opening verses of John 4, we see Jesus take an action we could call a withdrawal inspired by strategic compassion. He retreated to Sychar.

He stayed true to his purpose of caring about the best interests of the Pharisees, while freeing himself of unwanted drama. As he did so, Jesus's heart remained open to communicate with someone ready to hear his beautiful message. Jesus's choice to withdraw offers us much insight on choosing our own priorities.

How do we know when it's time to withdraw? First, consider what's best for the other person. Perhaps, the other person needs time to ponder a new perspective. Second, if your patience is also wearing thin, then it's probably time to regroup before you say something you regret.

STRATEGIC COMPASSION IN ENGAGEMENT

Strategic compassion can also include engaging those who are ready to meet with us in responsive ways. This can be refreshing to our souls. John 4:4 says, "He needed to go through Samaria."

Was this a side journey to seek out this beloved woman at the well? Perhaps he made a special trip to Samaria just for her.

Rather than getting frustrated when a person fails to hear, we may need to take a break, as Jesus did with the Pharisees. Then, we can switch gears to engage someone who is ready to hear. This engagement may be our most rewarding, refreshing strategy.

WHEN LEADERS FAIL TO HEAR

We've likely all been in situations where we felt no one listened or cared. For reasons beyond our control, sometimes our efforts meet with disdain, persecution, or bullying. Take heart, though. Negative responses often prove our ideas are being heard.

Sometimes, we need to practice patience as leaders process new information. Having tried and failed to reach others, strategic compassion may include retreat and prayer. In those cases, rest assured, consequences naturally unfold to correct those who refuse to hear. Take, for example, a situation when a leader of a Christian organization refused to hear my serious concerns about policies.

With my hands on my hips and my feet planted in a powerful stance, I looked up at this giant of a man. All around us, people passed by. They glanced over, trying not to stare. My mind raced with how to extricate myself from a confrontation. Oh my! How do I get myself into these messes?

I had tried many approaches with the leadership team before that day, hoping to call attention to ingrained problems with simple solutions. I tried several strategies to gain credibility for my perspective. I volunteered, offered free media consulting, brought food, and made a donation. I asked good questions, another gentle strategy to hold leaders accountable. However, good questions can also stir up the defense mechanisms of insecure leaders. On this day, yet again, I found myself in an awkward conversation with this leader.

The organization suffered from bullying and hazing throughout the ranks, in addition to some other communication blind spots. Because the adult leaders seemed blind to their own bullying tactics, they also tolerated hazing as part of their tradition. Consequently, other policy issues went unaddressed because people feared the leadership's response.

In addition, an existing policy within their framework allowed adult leaders to be alone with young people— something I think is a serious concern. Not only were the leaders of this organization too idealistic about the integrity of their staff, they did not want obvious dangers pointed out. At a minimum, with no accountability in place, leaders faced a serious threat of false accusations.

As a person who respected this organization, my conscience wouldn't rest until I spoke to the issue. If you've ever assumed you'd be heard, you may chuckle at my naïveté. Pointing out the truth about the issue of bullying and hazing got me labeled as a troublemaker.

I tried to offer help, yet again, in whispered, but urgent tones. I felt alone as I looked up at the tall man towering over my personal space. This leader, a kindhearted person in general, shut down honest feedback within his domain, but still thought he was a devoted listener. With his dogged stance on the perfect health of the organization, he successfully bullied everyone around him into silence about specific issues.

His mid-level managers, who should have felt free to offer solutions, were especially frustrated and forced into a passive-aggressive stance about systemic problems within the organization. Because I knew there was no hope of getting through his defenses at that moment, I decided to withdraw from our conversation.

"You don't have to always stage an intervention," one wise friend commented with a chuckle when I asked for advice.

My friend is right. Cutting the conversation short can extend your net pure influence in the long run. Unfortunately, not long after our conversation in the hall, there were public, legal accusations involving a member of their staff.

Whenever we refuse to hear, consequences follow. Leaders easily become entrenched in their own ideas, unwilling to hear anyone else's. Sometimes we may feel a leader adopts the leadership style of the Pharisees.

In daily, local news, we hear of heartbreaking and completely avoidable situations resulting from leaders who refuse to hear.

Setting Yourself Up for Success

When you choose to engage, you must set yourself up for success. Begin by establishing some healthy boundaries. For instance, you can limit the time set aside for a conversation. It's okay to space conversations out by asking for more time to pray and ponder before you talk again.

Besides setting up time limits, you can also negotiate specific boundaries ahead of time. For instance, no yelling or name calling allowed. Establishing common courtesy sets you up for victory when you engage strategically.

"Secure your partner's agreement to have a serious discussion. If your partner doesn't want to fight right now, you should set a time in the very near future. At first, you may encounter resistance and may have to be very persistent to set a definite time," say the authors of *Messages: The Communication Skills Book*.[2]

Messages also includes eight rules of fair fighting, which I find helpful:

1. Set a time.
2. State the problem.
3. Stick to one issue.
4. Express the full range of feelings.
5. Propose change.
6. Describe consequences.
7. Prevent escalation.
8. End in agreement, counterproposal, or postponement.

These rules of engagement are excellent standards of conduct for every conversation. Ideally, we want to be influencers who rarely get pulled into a fight or argument. If you find

interested in our little concerns when he has the whole universe to run?

Those are all good questions, and the answer is oh-so-simple. *Prayer is nothing more than a two-way conversation with God. Really. It's that simple.* His answers can be as soft as a whisper, as subtle as a coincidence, or as crucial as a heartbeat in the ICU.

Of course, many of us enjoy praying in community with others. We have experienced the power of corporate prayer when God answers his people together in a special way. However, prayer is essentially an individual practice. For example, a husband and wife can enjoy a meal out with other couples, but the intimacy of their individual relationship is special.

In the same way, God draws us into a uniquely individual intimacy, knowing each of us as he does. Conversational prayer becomes a special way of communicating with each one of his beloved children.

God waits eagerly to communicate with us. He wants to hear our concerns. One way we can "hear" God's heart is by responding to truth we find in Scripture. He loves to answer our prayers. All this because the God of the universe desires companionship with each of us and seeks us out. His own disciples reported that they proclaimed all about Jesus so we, too, could be his companions.

Perhaps the whole reason God made us to be natural communicators can be summed up in two ideas: 1. God wants to be our constant, loving companion, and 2. God wants us to have human companionship of the warmest, tenderest variety.

I'm not assuming we always know how to ask for or get the answers we want. We might not pray well at all. We may talk way too much and seldom listen. No matter, God's own spirit prays for us. He's not asking us to be perfect in prayer or anything else. Instead, we're invited into a sacred conversation with him through prayer in the most relaxed, refreshing way.

THE QUEST TO BECOME COMMUNICATION NINJAS

Some conversations are more difficult, just like some prayers take more out of us than others. In my quest to adopt Jesus's amazing communication tools and strategies, I searched for examples in the New Testament. Joyfully, I share them with you. They come with a warning label, though. Beware! When you practice them at home, your family catches on too.

I started trying out these strategies years ago in my own little test lab—my own family. Now, my husband and our kids use them on me too. That's kind of weird, and, yes, a little humbling, especially when I'm the one failing to hear those I love. The good news is, whenever I put aside my pride, it turns out these strategies work well, no matter who uses them.

All these years later, I am still learning to trust God and rest in his leadership. Maybe, like me, you've discovered the power of rest.

WHY RESTING IN SELF-CARE MATTERS

Like Jesus, there are times when we need to retreat to rest. Rest gives us time to recharge, refocus, and reprioritize. Jesus was the greatest teacher and the most loving man the world has ever known. Jesus secured time for his own rest and so must we.

He didn't abandon those who were not ready. Instead, he planted ideas and gave those ideas time to proliferate. Then, he strategically chose to engage with people who were ready to hear his message. All along the way, he rested in peaceful knowledge that he was in direct obedience to his Father.

Indeed, some people still failed or refused to hear Jesus. I find that thought comforting. Jesus came into this world to initiate a relationship with each person who chose to hear him. Yet, people rejected him despite his efforts and his own death and resurrection. Therefore, when our best efforts fail, we are not alone. Jesus understands the pressures we face as we try to knit our families together in life-long fellowship.

Isn't it true? We know what everyone else in the family needs but couldn't begin to tell anyone else what we need. For myself, self-care has been a moving target. These days, self-care includes marking off uninterrupted time to study and write, part of my own personal mental and spiritual health regimen.

Then, when I really want to give myself a break, I read historical fiction. You know what I mean—the fun stuff where I can enjoy and learn without any of my own brain power required.

How do you relax and unwind? Since self-care is one of those topics most women struggle to incorporate into their lives, I wanted to include a quick checklist for you here.

1. Sleep. Are you getting the sleep you need? Probably not. We all know the kids' costumes get made and deadlines get met at midnight after everyone else is asleep. Please schedule an early evening or a nap.
2. Healthy Food. By way of confession, I just ate nachos (nachos!) because I'm, um, too busy writing to take care of myself. Pray for me.
3. Clothing. I used to cheat myself on this one, but I've discovered I feel so much better if I respect myself enough to stay fresh on a new purchase each season. Nothing extravagant, just cute, functional, and comfortable. (Read: no tight sleeves.)
4. Exercise. Why not do something simple like walk around the block today or tomorrow? Do it for those who love you.
5. Companionship. Who in your life qualifies as a trustworthy friend who listens with mutual respect?
6. A Job Well Done. What are you working on currently to move yourself along educationally and professionally? Give yourself credit for your successes along the way, even if no one else notices the small stuff.
7. Still Moments Before the Lord. This one might be most important. (Although the next one is crucial too.) When she came on our show, Michelle Medlock Adams claimed to have the most sanctified SUV on the planet because she is constantly talking to the Lord as she drives along.[3] Time with God doesn't have to be complicated, but it needs to be honest and, in Michelle's case, often hilarious too.
8. A Grateful Heart. Gratitude is an energizing fuel for accomplishing all God has for us. More on that in the

next chapter. I can't wait. You could say I'm grateful to get to write more about gratitude.

9. Freedom. Resting in the Lord means trusting him to be bigger than our challenges. Sometimes, we simply must take a minute to breathe without feeling guilty about it. As women we must feel free to put the oxygen mask on ourselves first, like on an airplane.

If you look over my quick checklist, and you're firing on four or five cylinders out of nine, then you are rocking self-care. In fact, you're taking such good care of yourself, you can add number six to your list automatically, since clearly your self-care is a job well-done. I'm proud of you! Self-care is a form of self-compassion and honors God's love for us.

If resting was essential to Jesus, how much more so for us? When folks we love fail to hear us, compassion and companionship may require us to circle back and try again later. In the meantime, we can withdraw and rest, while engaging with those who are ready to mutually hear and share.

We owe it to ourselves to be the champion communication ninjas God intends us to be. Self-compassion requires we build rest into our lives, just as Jesus did. Strategic compassion equips us to be influential people indeed. The line for Communication Ninja-hood forms here, and we don't have to throw a single piece of Tupperware.

BEST QUESTION ABOUT STRATEGIC COMPASSION

How do we develop strategic compassion?

As much as we want to help everyone who has needs, we can't. We grow weary trying. Plus, discussions with people who can't hear are often counterproductive, even argumentative. Those discussions waste precious time we could use to rest or engage with folks who are ready.

Communication requires serious skills—it's not for the fainthearted. We are warriors—ninjas willing to fight for fellowship in our families. To be influential, our focus must be to share whatever wisdom we have with those mutually ready to exchange it. We must learn to value the rest provided by trusting God. He gives a gentle nudge about when to withdraw for a while and when to engage.

I've tested all the tools and strategies in this book. I wish I could tell you they all work one hundred percent of the time. However, tools and strategies may be effective one time and fail the next. Circumstances constantly change.

To be a communication ninja, we need to train our hearts in a habit of compassion. Then, we are always ready when opportunity presents itself. With skill and patience, we also get good at judging when it's time to walk away with our dignity intact. You know, before we start throwing Tupperware.

PRACTICAL TIP: HEAR GOD

Today, simply get before God on your knees and listen. Don't talk and don't ask for stuff. Don't fret about how weird the whole prayer and knees thing might feel. Simply listen. Open the Bible and ask God to help you understand his Word for your circumstances today. It's okay to be quiet before God. Then, if you decide you want to whisper a prayer to him in the midst of the quiet, he hears.

If you don't fall asleep (which Jesus's disciples did, by the way), then pat yourself on the back for trying something really special. Easy peasy.

We often get confused when it comes to prayer. For instance, we go to God with a thousand requests, but we fail to observe his responses. Today, let's give God the go-ahead to exercise pure influence in our hearts by listening for his voice. We can do this easily by reading the Scriptures often. If we do so, his voice will be the one we hear in our minds and hearts. Then, our readiness and his compassion will qualify us to be people of pure influence in this messy world.

MAY WE PRAY TOGETHER?

Dear Father in heaven, you love us and desire to teach us all we need to know for today. What a miracle that you care so much for us. You make yourself available to give us your undivided attention and listen to our prayers. It's so easy to get discouraged when people reject our ideas or fail to hear. But if we choose to be quiet before you, you will hear our solitude. Thank you, Lord.

Teach us to be responsive and careful in our conversational adventures. Give us patience as we trust you. Help us to be qualified by our ready hearts, even when we feel unqualified. Teach us strategic compassion. Allow us to learn from your beloved Son when to withdraw and when to engage. Help us listen well without assumptions. Help us know when it's time to take a break and rest. Encourage our hearts as we develop the habit of pondering. Teach us how to grow as people of pure influence. Bless us now because that's your heart's desire. In Jesus's name. Amen.

"Don't underestimate the value of doing nothing, of just going along, listening to all the things you can't hear, and not bothering." —A. A. Milne

CHAPTER 3:
OVERCOMING SHORT CIRCUITS TO ENERGY

WHAT IS REQUIRED FOR BREAKTHROUGH CONVERSATIONS?
PEACEFUL, PURPOSEFUL PATIENCE.

> So He came to a city of Samaria which is called
> Sychar, near the plot of ground that Jacob gave to
> his son Joseph. Now Jacob's well was there. Jesus
> therefore, being wearied from his journey, sat thus
> by the well. It was about the sixth hour. (John 4:5–6)

Eleven o'clock at night was the magic hour. Throughout our years of parenting, one of our kids could be counted on to start talking at bedtime. Not my bedtime, mind you, which is much earlier. Instead, right before she dropped off to sleep at 11:00 p.m., one of our daughters would readily share all the juicy details of her life and heart. If I wanted to connect with this amazing young person, I had to stifle my yawns and listen late.

Some of the best stuff seems to happen when we are bone tired. We fight exhaustion constantly as we attempt to meet needs in our messy world. How do we manage all we have to do and still connect in those "big stake" moments? The key to gaining influence boils down to peaceful, purposeful patience. That's a lot of p's, but here goes.

Don't you just hate being patient? I sure do. In this chapter, we'll take a close look at

- how to reestablish peace in our hearts,
- the way Jesus made the most of waiting moments with purposeful energy, and
- how impatience conveys disdain, but patience is synonymous with love.

REESTABLISHING PEACE IN OUR OWN HEARTS

Patience is so much more than waiting in line politely. Patience commits to the long haul in relationships. Establishing peace in our own hearts frees up energy for others. Therefore, it's essential for us to examine the things most likely to short-circuit our energy for patience. Two insidious drains on our emotional energy are guilt and shame.

We don't often hear teaching on the purpose of guilt and shame in our lives. Consequently, we don't always deal with our God-designed emotions in healthy, constructive ways. Yet, when we do, we free up valuable emotional energy. Emotional energy is a godsend.

We all may feel ambushed by guilt and shame sometimes. Maybe a child reminds us of a costume we forgot to make. Or our husband comes home from work with bad news, and we secretly rejoice we no longer must plan a dinner party. Or we prepare the best Sunday school lesson of our life but feel hurt and angry when our teaching partner torpedoes our ideas, and then feel guilt and shame about our anger.

Guilt and shame are common emotions. They sap our energy if we let them. When we view guilt and shame in a healthy way, however, we learn to release ourselves from distractions and foolishness. This, in turn, allows us energy to practice patience with compassion and joy.

To be patient with others, we must learn to be patient with ourselves first.

GUILT AND SHAME ARE NOT THE SAME

Some have described guilt as an inner personal experience, while shame is an outward experience of how we think the world sees us. They say guilt is what we feel when we've done something we believe is wrong. Shame is when we think others may perceive us as unworthy.

In my experience, guilt is the short-term emotion, and shame is the long-term one. God designed both with his purpose in mind. True guilt says, "Gee, I'm sorry I made that mistake and now my family will suffer with me while I try to make up for it." True shame says, "I'm sorry I have nurtured a bad attitude and now that habit is coming back to bite me. Despite my feelings of unworthiness, I will seek help to make changes one day at a time."

The single purpose of both guilt and shame (and all our emotions) is to keep us healthy in our relationships, especially in our relationship with God.

GUILT: THE QUICK TRIGGER

Guilt is energy for immediate change. The powerful emotion of guilt triggers quick action to make things right in a healthy person with appropriate self-respect. When we feel healthy guilt, our emotions are telling us we've harmed another person. Guilt spurs us to seek mercy.

If we immediately take responsibility for hurting ourselves or another person, we instantly feel relief. In this sense, guilt and shame both are fuel to keep us highly functional in our most important relationships.

Of course, every person has momentary glitches when self-indulgence beats out self-discipline. We may stubbornly refuse to apologize because we don't want to admit we messed up. Once we embrace our responsibility to get right with those we love, we then can let go of guilt and shame. In those moments, the temporary purpose of guilt and shame has accomplished the mission.

SHAME: THE LONG-TERM FUEL

Although closely related, shame is different from guilt. Healthy shame develops when we've made ongoing bad choices or adopted poor attitudes contrary to our own moral values. God's word is a compelling way to establish personal moral codes. Like long-term physical pain, shame lets us know something is not working correctly in our life. If we make habitually selfish choices, we may experience true shame. Shame is a healthy response to our own habitual bad attitudes and choices.

For instance, we may feel ashamed if we fail to serve our own parents as they age. Nowhere is confusion about shame more likely than when it comes to caring for our aging parents. I find myself leaning on my children these days, but it wasn't too long ago when I learned to establish boundaries with my dad.

We spent many happy days of my childhood helping in the yard, especially raking the leaves. As my dad aged, he began to count on me and my growing kids to fill in around his yard and garden. It was a pleasure, but we had our own house to keep up with too. As his health began to fail, more and more of my time was spent helping Mom get him to doctor's appointments. Finally, with much regret, I learned to draw a boundary with Dad about the yard.

"Dad, is that a job someone else can be paid to do? I really want to use my time to be there for the things only a daughter can do."

On one hand, if our parents ask us to meet any need they should responsibly handle on their own, we may feel a sense of false shame when we decline. On the other hand, healthy shame may fuel us to resolve old conflicts with our parents as their health begins to fail.

All the while, we must remember our parents may have made poor choices along the way that are beyond our responsibility. Even though we may suffer with them as they experience the consequences of their past decisions, we need not adopt false shame over their decisions.

THE QUICK FIX, BUT WHO SAID ANYTHING ABOUT EASY

When we recognize we are truly guilty of hurting someone else, the simple solution is to ask for forgiveness. We ask God for forgiveness and instantly receive his mercy, provided by Jesus's death and resurrection. We may have to patiently wait while another person forgives us, though. No one said forgiveness was easy.

When we feel truly ashamed, we must begin by recognizing our pattern of self-destruction. Next, we pray to God for forgiveness and help. Then, we ask forgiveness from those who have been hurt by our selfish habits. We may need to enlist help to make changes. We can ask trusted friends to hold us accountable for attitudes that lead to destructive patterns.

I experienced this as a young woman when I realized my dating habits were unhealthy and self-destructive. I felt ashamed of habitual decisions I made. To give myself time to develop healthy self-respect, I decided to quit dating altogether for several years. True and appropriate shame was my friend, motivating me to pursue a new, healthy way of thinking and living.

The discomfort of healthy shame motivated me to seek answers from the Scriptures about spirituality. Once I began to practice a new mindset—called the mind of Christ in the Bible—I began to free myself of residual shame. I practiced telling myself the truth that since Jesus died for me, I was worthy of respect. In my life, healthy shame was fuel for long-term changes that took a lot of energy and courage. Therefore, healthy shame was a manifestation of God's grace in my life.

AN APOLOGY: A POWERFUL CONVERSATION

I reached my sin quota long ago. Now, when I mess up, I try to apologize quickly. It simply takes too much energy to have important relationships off-kilter for too long. In a healthy person with appropriate self-respect, the powerful emotion of guilt triggers quick action to make things right with others. We make things right in a special conversational adventure—an apology. Such a simple concept, yet such a difficult conversation.

Even though they may seem difficult, apologies set the universe back in order. We receive God's mercy by asking him for forgiveness. When guilt prompts us to ask another person for forgiveness, we declare to the world we trust in God's redeeming mercy. We are free to rejoice because God's grace and mercy are magnified when we keep our relationships in proper order.

Sometimes people fail to forgive us even when we ask. In those cases, we can rest knowing we were honest about the wrong we inflicted, especially when we've tried to make amends to the best of our ability. By asking for forgiveness, we shift responsibility back to the other person for their decision to forgive or live with unforgiveness. We are free to patiently trust God with their response.

WAITING WITH PURPOSEFUL ENERGY

As Jesus rested, he was in no way subject to guilt or shame of any sort. If only that could be our experience! Instead, we are subject to guilt and shame, plus we must figure out when we are being guilted or shamed into doing stuff we don't want to do. Even stuff we absolutely should not do. No wonder we feel sapped of energy!

Jesus patiently conversed with the woman at the well. He gave her the time and attention she needed to resist and test him. Oh, to be so peaceful in our conversations! We must free ourselves of false guilt and false shame. Then, we can rest and wait with the same purposeful energy Jesus demonstrated with the woman.

We may feel false guilt and false shame simply because we don't understand boundaries and proper etiquette. False guilt results when we take on responsibilities that are not ours. We adopt false shame when we fail to embrace our own humanity. In other words, when we habitually fail to meet our own unrealistic expectations.

False guilt says, "I am obligated to do something for another adult, even though that person is perfectly capable." False shame says, "I can't believe I left my purse at the restaurant again. I must be a total loser. How can I be so forgetful all the time? I don't deserve to have friends and family." (That last example about the purse might or might not be a real example from my life. Ouch!)

Another example of false guilt is when we feel guilty about failing to help a neighbor in his yard. The yard work is his, not ours. If we pledge to help him, then fail to follow through, a quick apology should leave us guilt-free.

On the other hand, real guilt may be excellent fuel to nudge us to clean up our own yard. In fact, if we let our yard get really awful, we may start feeling legitimate shame about our ongoing failure to respect the neighborhood's best interests. Our long-suffering neighbors may be relieved when healthy guilt and shame finally converge to motivate us to work in our own yard.

FALSE GUILT AND FALSE SHAME: A BILLBOARD FOR IMPATIENCE

False guilt and false shame remind me of the brightly lit billboards on the highway near my home advertising the virtues of local attorneys in larger-than-life glory. I know their specialties based on their ads. In the same way, false guilt and false shame are an advertisement for a person's impatient need to coerce people and control an outcome.

One of the greatest distractions to effective communication is impatience. Impatience is death to relationships. Therefore, let's look at how coercing or controlling others with impatience, expressed in false guilt and false shame, can derail our influence.

I recently witnessed a leader indulge in a mini temper tantrum before a crowd of about sixty wholehearted volunteers. While she didn't pitch a fit like a toddler, her adult tactics still qualified as a temper tantrum. From the front of the room, she complained about how slowly the project was moving. Sadly, many of the volunteers were working hard, even donating money to the project. Yet, the leader omitted this truth without acknowledging it.

This was a big departure from her usual way of honoring individuals and expressing her thanks publicly. Because problems will sometimes arise within an organization due to volunteers, what options do leaders typically have at their disposal?

To avoid false guilt and false shame, a leader can easily hold individuals accountable privately. It may also be necessary to address group dynamics by bringing in a facilitator trained to identify problems and reunite the team. When trying to motivate a group of volunteers, gratefulness goes much farther than false guilt and false shame to speed up a project. Plus, it's always a good idea to keep reiterating the big vision and invite volunteers to "own" the project by contributing ideas and time, as well as money.

Instead, this leader chose to scold the organization's best volunteers. In her impatience, she put her drive for quick results over the best interests of the long-term project. By doing so, her relationship with her volunteers took a hit too.

Hers was a rookie mistake that's easily corrected. When our impatience gets the best of us—expressing itself in temper tantrums—finding a seasoned leader to lovingly mentor us could be as simple as a quick phone call. There are life coaches in abundance, not to mention trained church staff members who fearlessly help others. Most importantly, the Bible is a source of inspiration for leaders who wish to thrive.

Whoever uses false guilt and false shame as motivators loses in the long run. As leaders, we instantly become more effective by taking a moment to consider how patiently Jesus inspired the woman at the well. Guilt and shame help us work on healthier relationships. False guilt and false shame have the opposite effect.

ACCIDENTAL IMPATIENCE

Leaders get off track by pushing an agenda without patiently hearing others' perspectives. Most of us are guilty of this, whether at home, work, or church. When we become impatient as we press toward our goals, we quickly lose influence. Impatience can catch us by surprise even though it's easy to identify and diagnose.

Take, for instance, the way false guilt and false shame permeated the regular greeting I received from my grandmother. See if you hear the impatience I recognized in her voice.

Every Tuesday morning, I loaded up my adorable daughters to go visit her. I packed their bottles, pacifiers, and spare clothing and lugged the diaper bag. Huffing and puffing, I shepherded two little ones through the parking lot and into the assisted living home. We arrived in an explosion of lovable toddler cuteness, overflowing with their enthusiastic hugs and slobbery kisses.

"Where have you been? I haven't seen you in days!"

She always greeted me the same way each Tuesday, even when I made special trips in between. I knew she loved me and my kiddos. She loved our visits.

I was functioning at full capacity. I needed words of encouragement. She didn't mean to load me up with false guilt for what I was failing to do, i.e., visit more frequently. Finally one day, I responded in the gentlest way I could manage.

"Meme, will you greet me by saying, 'I'm so glad to see you' instead of the way you normally do?"

Meme didn't intentionally pile on the false guilt. She just wanted me to visit daily, hourly ... a lot. Instead of allowing the false guilt and false shame to get to me, I gave her suggested wording to help us both feel more loved.

IMPATIENCE AND DISDAIN ARE SYNONYMS

Subjecting others to habitual impatience communicates disdain and can affect others' self-worth. Patience is required to practice the gentle art of companionship in all our relationships. Patience is especially crucial to children and grandchildren. Nothing builds security and value in the hearts of those we love like patience.

If gentle patience is the surest way to build self-worth in others, then what are the consequences of habitual impatience? Insecurity, false guilt, permeating shame, anxiety, and an unwholesome drive to be perfect are the close companions of impatience. In fact, many parents inadvertently coach their children to assume false shame for others' dissatisfaction, thus undermining their children's confidence.

When we lose our patience, we short-circuit our own energy. Plus, we communicate an unintentional message. Impatience says we don't love the other person enough to slow down and engage with love. One impatient comment powerfully conveys oodles of disdain. A habit of impatience does lasting damage.

As we release ourselves from a sense of pervasive false guilt and false shame, we become more sensitive to those emotions in others. Awareness opens opportunities to practice patience. We can't force others to listen. As much as we may want to draw out authentic conversations, we simply must wait patiently for others to engage.

Like the leader who needed to give her volunteers a chance to buy in by contributing their own ideas to the vision she presented, sometimes we must wait for others to see the value of conversational adventure we want to have together. In the meantime, we can express our love for others by patiently and courageously giving them the information and time they need to process.

PATIENCE: LOVE IN SOFT SLIPPERS

Noticing how patiently Jesus focused on the woman and introduced ideas to her, we immediately recognize the truth of 1 Corinthians 13: "Love is patient." We may assume patience is one of many adjectives describing love.

My sweet mom had tiny feet. For Christmas one year, we bought her a pair of moccasins, lined in soft sheep fur. We thought she would wear them at home, like bedroom slippers. Instead, she wore them everywhere and collected them in all colors for every outfit. Mom liked warm toes.

Patience is love in soft, warm slippers. Like Mom's slippers, when we put on patience, we wrap our love around the other person. Patience is not a single aspect of love but love's whole aspect. Why? Patience is the perfect expression of love that does not reject—it accepts with the long haul in mind.

Patience says we love the other person and value them. Jesus managed to pour out love to the woman at the well, expressed in supreme patience in a moment when he was weary. He did not let distractions lead him astray, even in his own weariness. Instead, he focused on his priority—to engage her in an effective conversational adventure. We renew our own joy and energy as we communicate to others how dear they are to our hearts.

A MODEL OF GRACE

Patience is a sweet expression of love. Often other good attitudes, including self-compassion, follow closely behind granting patience to ourselves and others. By cutting yourself some slack, you model grace for those you love.

For a quick, yet in-depth, review of how mighty grace is in our lives, I recommend Nancy Kay Grace's book, *The Grace Impact*.

In it, she writes about hearing the words of 2 Corinthians 5:17 for the first time, "'Therefore, if anyone is in Christ, the new creation has come: The old has gone the new is here!' Those words penetrated my mind and went straight to my heart. My soul stirred with awareness of God's presence reaching out to me. When I found the passage in the Bible, the words jumped into my empty heart. I received His acceptance, forgiveness, and love. I traded my sin-stained self-image for one that reflected the image of the loving God. The holy, exalted God of the universe extended grace to me, and I gratefully took hold of it."[1]

Grace is a beautiful picture of God's loving patience extended toward us. Grace is what God gives us as he waits for us to figure out we need his mercy. Mercy is the quick fix to guilt. Grace is God's long-term commitment to empower us to rid ourselves of shame-producing bad habits.

We may need all the grace we can get to pass on to folks in our own families who drive us bonkers. Perhaps, like Jesus with the woman at the well, as we converse with someone we love, the person offers many objections. As we proceed, we'll see the way Jesus initially ignores the woman's objections then circles back to handle them with understanding, patience, and compassion.

GRATITUDE FUELS PATIENCE

When it comes to filling our own bucket, one other important resource for emotional energy is gratitude. We may be tempted to focus on past failures or future desires. However, when we discipline our hearts to be grateful in our current circumstances, patience often comes more easily.

Maybe, like me, you have a sense of God's purpose in your life, and you need energy for the life he gives you. For people like us, gratitude is our secret weapon in spiritual battle.

Gratitude might be the most energizing force in the universe. No wonder God likes to hear the praises of his people. What else could energize us so well for the purpose he has for us today?

When we consider all the ways God blesses us, we begin to develop gratitude for his design of each one of us. Joyfully, we understand he loves us and wants us to take care of ourselves, as we saw in chapter two. When we are full of impatience, we demonstrate disdain for ourselves and others. Patience is another important part of self-care.

Self-care is one way we express gratitude to God. Self-patience and self-compassion, for instance, remind our hearts God is aware of our frailties and loves us. His love is proof we are worthy of love and respectful treatment. Patience for ourselves also fuels patience for others. Like Jesus took care of himself by resting, we, too, must embrace self-care, expressed in self-patience and self-compassion.

Letting go of past mistakes frees up energy for today. Jesus's death on the cross proves forgiveness is available to those who choose it. Forgiveness, patience, compassion, and gratitude are closely linked. In forgiveness, we find a profound way of self-care and a beautiful path to gratitude.

Best of all, gratitude revs us up. Gratitude is like the blueberry super food of the emotional world. Patience and gratitude are best friends. The kind of patience we want in all our relationships is the kind Jesus offered the woman, allowing her to reach her full potential for influence. Imagine the burst of joy he felt to see her influence her whole community.

WAITING? WHO HAS TIME?

Patience takes energy and we all get weary. Putting aside false guilt and false shame allows us to retain more of our energy for patience, especially in those waiting moments we all experience. When our bucket (or jar like the woman at the well) feels empty, how can we fill it up again? Just when we think we can't manage even one more trip for water, we realize we better pull up a little more patience and save some energy for ourselves.

Indeed, sometimes we must cut ourselves a little slack, pouring out patience on our own souls. We do this with self-care, prayer, self-forgiveness, and self-compassion. Nothing saps our emotional energy like carrying around a bucket full of self-condemnation. We simply must develop a habit of patiently accepting the limits and frailties of our own human hearts. We must give ourselves freedom.

As we acknowledge God's goodness and grace toward us, we release ourselves from false guilt and false shame. Those negative emotions are replaced with gratitude. What pleasure to sit in his presence and absorb the beautiful truth of his unfailing love and devotion to each one of us.

Being patient may not be easy, but it's always good. Experiencing God's patience with me firsthand allows me to extend patience to myself and others. Perhaps you, too, have experienced the magnificent power in practicing patience through God's grace. Long haul relationships require patience, especially for our own sweet selves.

To be truly successful in using the tools Jesus demonstrated, we need to take multiple trips to the well for the Living Water of God's own Spirit. We need to keep refilling our patience buckets, by drawing deeply in our relationship with him.

With grateful hearts, we soon discover he refills our buckets. We can even ask others to help us, just like Jesus asked the woman at the well for a drink. In fact, when we ask for help, we may further expand our influence, as we will see in the next chapter. Simultaneously, we invite others to expand their influence as well. Now that is worth the wait.

BEST QUESTION ABOUT PATIENCE

When leaders impatiently scold you or use subtle threats, what can you know immediately about their motivations?

Scolding and threatening are about control and coercion. When a person uses extreme measures, like shaming employees, an impatient leader is simply using a motivation technique that often works. At home, because false guilt and false shame are often powerful motivators, parents frequently instill them in their kids. When these emotions become so entrenched in us as children, they may cripple us as adults. Later, we may have trouble noticing when someone falsely guilts or shames us to control or coerce us.

Sometimes we can offer gentle, corrective input in those moments. We may ask a simple question like, "What is the goal on this project?" or "What is our hearts' desire for our family?" to realign priorities and get the conversation back on track. Ironically, we may need to practice patience with our leaders.

We can note where our responsibilities begin and end when we identify false guilt and false shame. Thus, we develop healthy boundaries. Plus, we return to the source of our worthiness—Jesus. He provides energy for self-forgiveness and self-compassion. Energetic gratitude and joy become hallmarks of our life.

Fortunately, we have a wonderful example of gentle truth received in joyful gratitude in the beautiful story of the woman who found Jesus at the well. In the coming chapters, we will continue to dissect how the Savior, though weary, offered the woman patient respect and love without guilting or shaming her.

PRACTICAL TIP: TOUGH CONVERSATIONS

Make a list of recent tough, uncomfortable conversations. Now try to analyze why the conversations felt awkward. Ponder when guilt might have been healthy or false in each conversation. Then, list any healthy or false shame as well. For reference, ask yourself which decisions you made in the conversations. Your decisions are your responsibility. Here are some examples of great questions to help.

- Did I speak impatiently today, when I should have been patient, and therefore feel guilty?
- Is shame a legitimate feeling for me because I habitually speak harshly?

52

- If I am in the habit of hurting others with my words, is it time to let shame motivate me to practice patience in this area of my life?
- Do I feel guilty because I should have spoken up, instead of letting a bad situation go too far?
- Is avoiding confrontation an unhealthy habit for me, therefore I suffer chronic shame?

I hope your list is short. We don't need to beat ourselves up because we're not perfect enough. The opposite is true. What we want to do here is free ourselves from unnecessary baggage by simply recognizing what is our responsibility and letting all else fall by the wayside. Practice self-patience by giving your heart time to ponder.

MAY WE PRAY TOGETHER?

Dear Father in heaven, you are such a tender communicator, never manipulating our emotions. You are always truthful. We are sometimes tempted to try to control others. We feel impatient and want to press our agendas ahead. Please help us see when we need to refresh our own souls with rest. Conversely, when others try to control us, we feel angry. We may even feel false guilt and false shame poured onto us by others. Help us, O Lord, so we experience guilt and shame in a healthy way. May we trust you with these powerful emotions? Free us from false guilt and false shame. Allow us courage to take responsibility when we hurt others. Give us grace to freely release the rest. We need your strength and wisdom to make amends when needed. Teach us to be faithful and kind. We need patience and insight from you. Help us forgive ourselves and others. Set us free to love patiently. May our hearts rejoice in gratitude for you. Bless us, O Lord, because it's your heart's desire to do so. In Jesus's name. Amen.

"Patience is the companion of wisdom." —Saint Augustine

CHAPTER 4:
AN OFFER WE CAN'T REFUSE

HOW DO WE FOCUS ON REAL NEEDS?
BY UNDERSTANDING WHAT WE HAVE TO OFFER.

> A woman of Samaria came to draw water. Jesus said to her, "Give Me a drink." For His disciples had gone away into the city to buy food. Then the woman of Samaria said to him, "How is it that You, being a Jew, ask a drink from me, a Samaritan woman?" For Jews have no dealings with Samaritans. Jesus answered and said to her, "If you knew the gift of God, and who it is who says to you, 'Give Me a drink,' you would have asked Him, and He would have given you living water." (John 4:7–10)

The editor of a local paper called me one day to ask for my help.

"Cathy, we need you to serve on the festival committee. I know how much you love veterans, and we need you to help figure out how to serve them," she said. "Besides, I think it will be good for you."

I can't cry. It's too unprofessional.

"Thank you for asking me," I replied with joy, trying not to sniff. This thoughtful friend never mentioned my unraveling marriage. Instead, she gave me a perfect excuse to get out of the house and breathe. They needed my help. I would be serving veterans. Oh, what joy!

By inviting me to share my talents, she opened a whole new avenue of learning for me. Plus, she gave me a chance to reboot my mental health and add a spark to my marriage with fun things to talk over with David.

Like my gracious friend, asking someone for help may be a kind gesture, and the opening to a great relationship. Jesus begins his beautiful conversational adventure with the woman at the well by asking her for a drink. If we hope to be people of influence, we need to take note of how Jesus connects with this woman.

This story is typically taught as if the woman's reputation was a bad one. Yet, notice how Jesus paid attention to her needs, not her reputation. Instead of judging any past, misguided choices, he begins by focusing on what she can offer him. Then, he makes her an offer she can't resist. Jesus begins their conversation by

- asking for her help,
- understanding her real need,
- ignoring the objections she tossed his way, and
- tickling her imagination.

ASKING FOR HELP

Imagine her surprise when Jesus asks her for help.

Honestly, some obscure, submerged feminist side of me pops up, full of defensiveness and insecurity as I read this passage in Scripture. Jesus's helpers were gone, and this woman was the only one around, is that it? Did he take for granted she would draw the water? Maybe I would have gotten him a drink. Or, like her, I might have tested him. *What, just because I'm a girl, you want me to carry your coffee?*

Yet, I also see how Jesus emphasized her value to him by asking for her help first. He draws her in by acknowledging she has something he needs and extends dignity to her by doing so. Only then, after asking for her help, does he focus on what he can offer her. Then, by offering to serve her, he amplifies her significance.

Like Jesus, we must know what we need and what we can offer.

How odd that Jesus, the Son of the Almighty God, is asking her for help. Yet, all of us want to know we matter, we are significant, and we can offer something of value to others.

TRIPPING OVER QUALIFICATIONS (OR LACK OF THEM)

Often our own insecurities get in the way of knowing what we need or what we can offer. They cause us to focus on all the wrong things. It's so easy to trip over qualifications or lack of them. We become easily distracted when we attempt to figure out whether we're qualified to speak up. We may wonder what gives another person the right to say certain things to us.

Who does he think he is? Why should I serve him? Is that person cooler than me? I love a good question, but those are not the right ones.

Instead of being envious or competitive with my brothers and sisters in Christ, I want to trust God with his purpose for my life. I want to ask better questions. *How is that person gifted? How do we fit together in God's kingdom? Why has God allowed another influential person to cross my path?* Good questions can help us stay focused for great conversations.

Good, non-judgmental questions are our best bet for understanding the real needs of others. *How can I serve you? Is there anything I can do to encourage you today? Have you found a favorite verse in the Scriptures this week?*

Do folks always greet our good questions with joy? Absolutely not. Many times, people toss objections our way. We may start to feel unqualified. Let's look how the woman at the well checked out Jesus's qualifications and how he responded.

IGNORING OBJECTIONS TO STAY FOCUSED

The woman's defense mechanisms went into overdrive at Jesus's request for her help. She wanted to know more before she agreed to do anything for him.

He asks her for a drink, but she responds with a challenging question. Her question could be considered a defense mechanism. "'How is it that You, being a Jew, ask a drink from me, a Samaritan woman?' For Jews have no dealings with Samaritans" (v. 9). She grabbed for one of the most politically charged prejudices floating around in her society.

We all hate injustice and man-made divisions, especially when we find ourselves in the minority. However, what if we're grasping at political straws because we simply don't have the courage to connect with unconditional love and respect? Squabbling over political differences is one way of preventing people from getting too close. Perhaps this was the woman's goal—to keep Jesus at bay and to keep her secrets hidden.

Have you been subject to other people's prejudices? Some experiences birth a guarded protectiveness in our hearts. Have other people's past prejudices made you want to know where the next person stood? Whether it's Samaritans, racism, gun control, the environment, Christianity ... it seems we divide over it. What we really want to know about the other person is, *Can I trust you?*

Any possible conversation seems doomed before under-standing can develop when someone is hard-hearted, opin-ionated, or ready to reject us. However, Jesus beautifully handled all the woman's objections with an even hand. He simply ignored them. Instead, he focused on drawing her into a relevant, life-changing conversation.

"If you knew the gift of God, and who it is who says to you, 'Give Me a drink,' you would have asked Him, and He would have given you living water" (v. 10).

The woman at the well had her insecurities, like most of us. She immediately challenged Jesus, knowing Samaritans suffered a perceived lack of status among Jews. However, he dismissed her objection—essentially telling her she was missing the point. He ignored her objection to maintain focus on what was truly important. What a great strategy! If only, in the heat of the moment, we could remember this plan.

Jesus did the unexpected. Instead of launching into a debate-style response to her political prejudice, he ignored her defensive moves and remained focused on his goal. Oh, how I admire his tender approach.

GOTCHA MOMENTS

We may wonder how Jesus resisted giving this gal her comeuppance (as we say in Texas) with a big dose of gotcha. If only we could be more like Jesus in those moments when we know (or at least think we know) we're right.

"Gotcha" moments are tempting. They are also tricky. We can win the gotcha moments and still lose the battle for fellowship and unity in our families. We've all had moments when we felt ourselves losing focus in a conversation.

Sally's mind fogged over as her friend ranted on one of her favorite soap boxes. *Focus, Sally! Listen carefully.*

"He never listens to me!"

Could it be because you rant about the same stuff constantly and his mind goes numb?

"Your husband is a good man," Sally said gently. "Have you tried starting a different kind of conversation with him? I could help you figure out a better strategy."

Her friend's chin quivered. "I'm afraid to."

From there, Sally and her friend embarked on a truly life-changing conversational adventure.

I'm proud of Sally for resisting the urge to lecture, correct, or rant back. Personally, I find gotcha moments very tempting. I must remind myself: *God is all-knowing; Cathy is not.* Instead of winning debate points, our goal should be to engage the hearts of those we love, gently and effectively. We want to build fellowship in our long-term relationships. Fellowship is the gentle art of companionship.

Companionship, fellowship, and community are the long-range goals of all communication, not winning debate points. Besides, even if we win the debate, our credibility may take a dive. Why? True credibility comes from understanding the needs of those we love and being faithful to the call to serve each other.

CREDIBILITY CAN'T BE COUNTERFEITED

In today's world of immediate access to opinion with the click of a mouse button, credibility becomes essential. How do we exercise influence in a world searching for truth? Even with so many people claiming to be experts, we can learn to recognize true credibility. I like what Fred Smith, retired president of the Gathering, says on the topic of credibility.

> We think our accomplishments and wisdom will give us credibility, but it doesn't. Only one thing alone will answer that most basic question people have for us today. "How do we know the Lord has appeared to you?" What is it in our character, our spirit, our demeanor, and our actions that say to people who are cynical and hardened that we have been with the Lord? What is our sign for today that will say to people we are not just another wave of do-gooders, opportunists, ideologues, and partisans who have come on our own to do what we think is best?[1]

Fred talks about the way God established Moses's credibility among all the other folks claiming spiritual credentials in another part of this passage. Fred's point is well-made. True credibility can't be counterfeited—it must be a byproduct of integrity and authenticity.

If we want to influence our messy world, we must spend time getting to know the One who is loving and merciful and the embodiment of justice. Dogma and debates have no place in our conversations. We must open our hearts to consider the values and perspective of others.

How could Jesus ignore her legitimate concern? Because he understood her real needs better than she did. We may not be as perceptive as Jesus but distinguishing between irrelevant objections and real needs enhances all our conversations.

Jesus did not get into a theoretical, philosophical discussion of religious history, a hot topic. Nor did he debate politics. He simply focused on the real issue—her real needs. Jesus was confident in his purpose because he knew what he offered this woman.

UNDERSTANDING THE REAL NEED

Never was anyone more qualified than Jesus to meet the need of the human heart. When it comes to keeping the conversation relevant, Jesus expertly guides with a fabulous communication strategy. Jesus gives her the question he wants to answer.

"If you knew the gift of God, and who it is who says to you, 'Give Me a drink,' you would have *asked* him, and He would have given you living water'" (v. 10, italics mine).

You may want to try this. I use Jesus's strategy of suggesting the right question with my family. "Honey, I think you meant to ask, 'What can I do to help?'" It works like a charm if you say it with a wink and a smile. By suggesting the help I need, we avoid any hurt feelings in my kitchen.

Jesus suggested the very question to meet the woman's deepest need. He knew he could offer her exactly what she craved in the most sacred place of her heart. Her soul was supremely relevant to Jesus. He loved her enough to die for her. His objective was to serve her and her whole community. If only we could be more like him. Jesus respected her value and significance so much that he offered her something she could not refuse. Living water. With perfect insight, the Savior made his offer relevant to her life, sitting at the well where she came to draw water every day.

TICKLING THE IMAGINATION

"'If you knew the gift of God, and who it is who says to you ...'" With those words, Jesus gently whispered to her secret desire. In the deepest places of her heart, did she wonder if the coming Savior would care about her?

Perhaps you too desire intimate fellowship and companionship with the One who will accept, rather than reject. We were made for companionship—it's not good for us to be alone. It's safe to assume all people crave intimate fellowship in our most sacred hearts.

Jesus patiently helped her identify her real need with an outrageous idea. There was no way she would trust such an offer—yet. Surely this offer was too good to be true. Living water? However, he had piqued her curiosity. Her imagination stirred immediately. She wanted to know more.

What woman can resist a bargain? The idea of living water conveyed life flowing freely. This had to seem like a deal, especially to a woman who went to the well for water possibly multiple times a day. We can all wish for a life overflowing with ease. We love imagining a future where the house never needs repairs, we always love our job, the children grow up and have happy lives, our parents stay healthy without aging, and yes, even the pets live forever. If only life could be so easy.

I don't know about you, but I've had my share of vivid dreams. For instance, as a child, I was convinced I could fly. Upon waking up, I shared this tidbit of information with my younger siblings. I quickly realized—as they giggled hysterically—that flying was a figment of my slumbering imagination.

However, when my children were young, I offered them flying lessons on many a windy day. Flapping our arms and running down a long pier near our home, we tried often to achieve our imagination's ultimate goal. I can imagine how the Wright brothers felt when their bicycle took flight. Perhaps some dreams never take flight, but the dream of fellowship is within reach.

While we never got our feet off the ground for more than a leap, my children spent many happy days laughing and trying. Additionally, and this is important to a mommy, I never had to fish any flyers out of the lake on icy cold days. Ah, the glory of imagination when mixed with fellowship.

In the days before plumbing, Jesus might as well have offered the woman at the well a dishwasher. That idea would have seemed outrageous to her. If only such a thing existed.

Jesus opened the way to reach her heart by focusing on her real need. She needed a relationship with him. As he tickled her imagination, her objections transformed into interest.

The living water he offered came packaged in a metaphor of the real water she drew daily from the well where they sat. *If only the human heart's inner thirst could be quenched as easily as drawing up water from a well.*

Best of all, he freely offered her hope because he knew he could deliver what he promised. Fortunately, for us, we can offer the same hope Jesus offered—a relationship with him. In a world desperate for hope, our challenge is to spark imagination in those we love—to foster a thirst for eternal truth.

THE RIPPLE EFFECT OF COMMUNITY

Imagination starts in our homes where habitual kindness and respect train our children in a more judicious approach to conversation. Like a domino effect, as they grow up, our grown children practice more judicious conversations in our local communities. Additionally, real community, or unity, is fostered as people of varying perspectives feel heard, respected, valued, and catch a vision for living together peacefully. This influence of imagination is so powerful that it easily spreads from home to work to local communities and beyond.

Keeping in mind that this solitary woman went on to influence her whole community, I like what Gilbert Bilezikian wrote in his book, *Community 101.*

> Community is God's dearest creation because it is grounded in his nature and reflects his true identity as a plurality of persons in oneness of being. Moreover, the establishment of community was God's dream from the very beginning, and he pursued it all along through history and will continue to do so to the very end of time. This dream will be fulfilled when the church is ushered from time into eternity, to be united as a bride to her husband in the Savior's embrace of redemptive love.[2]

Since community and companionship are dear to God's heart, is it any wonder we long for them too? We label our churches, our neighborhoods, and even small towns as "communities." We even say our church is our "family." With that in mind, it becomes easy to see why Jesus sought out the woman at the well and why she ended up as such a person of influence. God is seeking to fulfill his own dream and he will use those who are ready to help him. Wow!

To expand our own pure influence for good and to keep our conversational adventures focused on real needs, we can take note of Jesus's strategies. We must keep in mind God's dream for us: tender companionship. Like him, we can ignore the objections others toss our way and instead tickle the imaginations of those we love.

Whether it's outrageously useful imaginary appliances, pier flying lessons, or any other silly idea you dream up, I hope you will use imagination like Jesus did. Please engage the imagination of those you love, prompting them to respond in positive, powerful ways.

BEST QUESTION ABOUT REAL NEEDS

How do we ignore those who test us with their prejudices and assumptions?

You don't have to take anyone's prejudices to heart. You may still never agree with the other person, but by listening respectfully you can understand another perspective better. For instance, social media today offers unique opportunities to listen, respect, and understand without responding. Responding is a choice.

Certainly, we are better off when we soak up various perspectives without making retaliatory comments, even when we need to speak up in the face of injustice. Our culture is in desperate need of judiciousness. By understanding the true value of our own experiences and insight, we can set the stage for respectful, open communication.

You will find your own imagination dreaming up creative ways to influence those you love for pure good as you understand the needs of others. We will look at more ways to spark imagination in the next chapter. And never forget, you can always ask your friends for help. One excellent way to come up with imaginative ideas is to ask for what you need. After all, Jesus began by asking for a refreshing drink of water.

PRACTICAL TIP: KNOWING WHO YOU ARE

Tonight, make a list of valuable things you are equipped to offer others. Sounds so easy and, yet, it's sometimes hard for us to take credit for anything. Like Jesus, do you notice when others' hearts are thirsty? Does your family love the way you remember important dates? Do you bring laughter to every situation? Are you a good cook? Are you able to share others' sorrows with empathy? Maybe our messy world doesn't value what you offer. Still, you know in your heart what you offer is valuable because sharing it gives you unfettered joy.

For the next hour, I hereby give you permission to extravagantly brag about every little cotton-picking thing you like about yourself. In Texas, we unashamedly brag about our state, our families, what we do, who we are, and, well, just about everything. Better get going, an hour isn't nearly enough time to write down all the things that are awesome about you!

Okay, I get it. Sometimes, we fail to give ourselves credit for so long, we forget how awesome we really are. If you're having trouble thinking of yourself in a grand way, start your list with the word "modesty." Boldness is probably near the top of my list, but it makes no difference where we fall in the personality spectrum. God has a perfect design for each of us, in all our glorious individuality.

Start your list and tape it on the fridge for a few days. Once your family figures out you're adding to your list of bragging rights, they may start to add suggestions on ways you're special. If they don't, no worries, just contact me on my website. I will send you a handy-dandy list to get you started. Lists are one of my specialties— I live to make lists— and you'll be doing me a favor by asking. Kind of like Jesus did for that nice lady at the well when he asked her for a drink.

MAY WE PRAY TOGETHER?

Dear Father in heaven, you made each one of us with a unique design created to bless those around us. As children of the King, we turn to you to remind us we are valuable simply because we belong to you. Together we say, "I am your child, a child of the Most High God, therefore beautifully and wonderfully made." We all get discouraged when someone fails to hear our insight. Please help us identify the ways you specifically equip us to be people of influence. Teach us what is relevant today for those we love. Grant us the ability to focus and to listen without being confused by distracting prejudices. Teach us to identify the real needs of others. Help us tickle the imagination of those we love with hope. Bless your child because that's your heart's desire. In Jesus's name. Amen.

"Prejudice is a great time saver. You can form opinions without having to get the facts." —E. B. White

CHAPTER 5:
IF ONLY? WHY NOT?

WHO DO YOU THINK YOU ARE?
WE CAN SIMPLY ENGAGE THE IMAGINATION OF OTHERS TO
CLAIM OUR CREDIBILITY.

> The woman said to him, "Sir, you have nothing to
> draw with, and the well is deep. Where then do
> you get that living water? Are you greater than our
> father Jacob, who gave us the well, and drank from
> it himself, as well as his sons and his livestock?"
> Jesus answered and said to her, "Whoever drinks
> of this water will thirst again, but whoever drinks
> of the water that I shall give him will never thirst.
> But the water that I shall give him will become in
> him a fountain of water springing up into everlast-
> ing life." (John 4: 11–14)

My grandparents lived in a frame house, built by my
great-grandparents in the 1800s in Austin, Texas. Each
bedroom had antique cabinets with chamber pots still in
them. My grandfather had to explain their function to me.
If you like touring historic homes, you probably know the
house's style. A hallway ran through the middle on each
of its two stories, dividing the rooms symmetrically. Floor-
to-ceiling windows on the end of each hallway provided
ventilation in hot Texas summers long before air condi-
tioning. Sadly, function preempted architectural form
when one end of the second-floor hallway was converted to

the house's only bathroom. But oh, the benefits of indoor plumbing.

I thank God for indoor plumbing every time I turn on the tap at my house and fill up a cold glass of clear, clean water. What Jesus said to the woman at the well about never being thirsty again sounds crazy, especially in the context of their cultural reality. Certainly, there would always be the unending trips to the well, right? How could endless water supply quench thirst forever anyway? Thirst returns.

Which leads us to an enlightening truth: All creative innovations start with imagination and the thoughts, *If only* and *Why not?* Authentic communication—drawing out deep conversations—requires that same kind of creativity and imagination.

Just as Jesus knew he could deliver what seemed beyond imagination, we must trust in our ability to deliver. How do we know we can deliver? What are our credentials? First and foremost, our credentials start with the relationship we have with our Savior.

Still, when it comes to our own credentials, we seem to lack imagination and confidence. Maybe we were told as a kid we'd never amount to anything and we still hesitate to try. We get stuck in old ways of thinking about what we can accomplish—or not accomplish. We may feel discouraged as people challenge our credibility. We may hit the roadblock of our own self-doubt even when we offer great, innovative ideas.

If only and *Why not?* Let's really home in on one of Jesus's most powerful strategies for claiming your influence and keeping your conversational adventures on track—the disciplined use of imagination.

The woman at the well challenged Jesus's credibility. She went so far as to suggest her community's credibility might be at least as good as his. We'll see how Jesus keeps engaging her imagination by

- addressing her challenge with confidence,
- choosing inclusion,
- using a handy visual aid, and
- continuing to spark her imagination with fresh ideas.

WHEN OTHERS CHALLENGE OUR CREDENTIALS

It seems like you spend hours, even days, preparing. You create a slide presentation. You dot every *I* and cross every *T*, sparing no research. You get a haircut and put on your most professional outfit. When the big day arrives, you make your presentation. In your heart, you're hoping *if only they get it.* Instead, you're shocked to discover your idea does not garner enthusiastic support. It feels like the rest of your team is asking, "Who do you think you are? What gives you the right to say that?"

Folks question our credibility constantly. What they really want to know is whether you are qualified and if they can trust you.

For those moments, I have great news. Truth stands on its own merit. Yet, communicating truth doesn't always guarantee other folks will like the message. Even so, like Jesus, we want to be faithful to deliver truth in the most creative ways we can imagine.

Who do you think you are? What a yucky question. The very question itself divides us into two groups—people who deserve respect and those who don't. Would you believe I've had leaders ask me that out loud? One time, I was so surprised I stood there stuttering. Finally, I simply responded, "I'm a human with a spirit." The man blinked a few times as he processed my unexpected answer. Like a toy soldier with stiff limbs, he quickly retreated with a lame excuse.

We're in good company when people challenge our credibility. In Jesus's case, the woman at the well went so far as to challenge Jesus personally. Her words could be rewritten to say, "Who do you think you are anyway?"

> The woman said to him, "Sir, you have nothing to draw with, and the well is deep. Where then do you get that living water? Are you greater than our father Jacob, who gave us the well, and drank from it himself, as well as his sons and his livestock?" (John 4:11–12)

First, the woman pointed out Jesus had nothing to put water in. It's a deep well, she said. With skepticism, she drilled him with insightful questions. *Living water? Really? So, who made you better than Jacob? Yep, we're experts about Jacob around here because he was our ancestor. What do you think about that, buster? Bam. Gotcha!*

THE CHALLENGE OF COMPETING CREDENTIALS

As the woman at the well challenged Jesus's credentials, she subtly emphasized her own. Perhaps, because she was unsure of the validity of her own status, she accentuated her community's claim instead. "Are you greater than our father Jacob, who gave us the well, and drank from it himself, as well as his sons and livestock?"

Hers was a rich and valid claim of credibility. We've all had moments where somebody in the room began to remind the group that their credentials were more impressive than ours. In fact, it can happen easily in any home between a husband and a wife. The woman at the well asserted her pedigree as a descendant of Jacob. This comes after she challenged Jesus on the prejudice of the day against Samaritans. For us to understand the significance of her comments, her claim is worth checking out.

For quick reference, God gave Abraham, Jacob's grandfather, a promise to bless lots of future generations through his children. Jacob, later named Israel, had twelve sons. All the twelve tribes came from Jacob's twelve sons, including son number four, Judah. These sons became the kingdom of Israel, until they split.

The Bible tells us that eleven of the tribes—minus the tribe of Judah—got off track and disobeyed God (2 Kings 17:7; 18:11; 21–25:21). Therefore, the king of Assyria captured the Israelites. The Assyrian conquerors carried the eleven tribes into exile. Consequently, for a moment in history, the tribe of Judah alone remained safe and somewhat faithful to God's plan for his people. Phew! That's a lot to process!

Eventually, God's patience ran out on the tribe of Judah's compromises, too, and they were also conquered. While under the authority of foreign powers, those living in Samaria, part of Israel, intermarried with their oppressors. Samaria got a bad rap with the other tribes who continued to follow the law of only marrying those from one of the twelve tribes. And you thought your family was messy.

While it may seem confusing, it boils down to one important fact for our purposes. The Jews (the descendants of Judah were often called Jews) thought they were better than the Samaritans. Why? The intermarrying of the Samaritans with non-descendants of Israel was the main thing. Plus, they shared a complicated political history which factored into the equation.

Despite lots more history up until Jesus's time, the Jews (in this context, the descendants of Judah) were still uppity when it came to their Samaritan neighbors. So, that's why the woman at the well challenged Jesus. For the Jews, being from Samaria became synonymous with being second-class from a religious and historic point of view, especially because of intermarriage.

When this beloved woman mentions Jacob's well, where they conversed, it's worth noting the validity of her community's historic significance. Here, at this very well, Jacob fell in love with his wife-to-be, Rachel. It's in this community that his father-in-law tricked him into first marrying Rachel's older sister, Leah. Eventually, he married Rachel too. Additionally, he took on two servant girls, impregnating them also, while living nearby.

The woman at the well circumvented all the history and drama that separated Samaritans from Jews and subtly reminded Jesus that Jacob is the father of all twelve tribes, which includes the Samaritans. She reminded him they shared the same ancestry. Thus, she laid claim to the same rich inheritance of God's promises to Jacob. Maybe she wondered if the Savior would reject the Samaritans like the Jews rejected them.

If only. If only this kind stranger will acknowledge my heritage.

Perhaps her confidence in this heritage prepared her heart to believe the coming Messiah would include her in his promises, despite the cultural prejudice of her day.

Why not? Why not ask this good stranger my hardest questions?

Her comments divide her from Jesus. However, Jesus is not drawn into her competition for who has the best credentials. We see how easily inclusion changes the tide of their conversational adventure. When others start a comparison about who has the best credentials, like Jesus, we can simply diffuse the competition by exerting inclusion.

Choosing Inclusion

Despite her claim to her community's A+ credentials, she still didn't grasp the truth Jesus is gently offering. Jesus, the master communicator, diffused all her objections with a single word: *Whoever*. In that one word (which he repeats), he blew away all her objections like breath on a dandelion. Poof! She was included, not rejected.

> "Whoever drinks of this water will thirst again, but whoever drinks of the water that I shall give him will never thirst. But the water that I shall give him will become in him a fountain of water springing up into everlasting life." (John 4:14)

The power of inclusion is highly underrated. Take, for instance, Shawn Ancor's observations in his book, *Before Happiness*, about the connection between inclusion and success:

> All it takes is consciously remembering that we need to include others in our reality. Remember, the reality you experience at work and at home is a constellation of meaningful facts that your brain has wrapped together. Finding meaning in the social support we give to others is one of the best ways to

harness our cognitive resources and intelligences to become more engaged, motivated, productive, and successful in our professional and personal lives.[1]

Including others is a conscious decision. Interestingly, by using the word *whoever*, Jesus also holds the woman accountable to make a personal decision. *Whoever* implies two things. First, there's a decision to be made. Second, inclusion is not based on human prejudice or credibility at all. He brings up a topic we still struggle to think and talk about today—eternal life. Now there's fodder for conversational adventure.

INCLUSION INVITES ACCOUNTABILITY

For a great example of how powerful inclusion can be, let me share a story involving my daughter Anna. Realizing I was without a guest for *Fireside Talk Radio* the week before Thanksgiving 2018, I buzzed my oldest daughter and asked her to co-host. Not only was it fun to do a show with such a talented and creative person, but I had another surprise for our audience. I was pretty sure we were nearing a million downloads at that point. What a big moment in the life of a newbie podcaster, especially a little old lady like myself.

Seconds before we went live, my tech guru whispered in my headphones that rather than one million downloads, we'd reached *two* million. At that point, I totally blanked. Anna told family stories, while I stuttered in surprise. Recovering, I asked the first question I could think of. What's your favorite childhood memory about Thanksgiving?

"I love the way we always included others," she answered.

Her answer was the biggest surprise of all on a show that went totally haywire. Here's why. I began inviting other folks to our family gatherings out of desperation, not because I was such a nice person. My frailty and sad heart prompted me to be inclusive, not my impressive spirituality.

Family holidays growing up for both David and I were family affairs with no guests. Both sets of our parents were hospitable every other day of the year, they just didn't think to invite anyone else over for family time at holidays. Once David and I began recognizing how dysfunctional we were, however, I began dreading family time. Life was uncomfortable for a while as we struggled to redefine our way of doing things together.

I started including anyone free to come to make family life easier and less strained. This changed the dynamic at holidays and insured we'd all be on our best behavior, especially David and me. As a bonus, inclusion became a way of life for us, a lifestyle our kids take for granted and, can you believe this, give me credit for.

I could never have planned such a spontaneous, fun show that day or anticipated the kind of kudos I got from a beloved daughter. The credit she gave me blossomed directly out of my frailty and dissatisfaction years ago. It's so beautiful to see my kids using inclusion every day as part of a fun lifestyle. My grandchildren enjoy the delight of surprise guests who bring spontaneous joy into our lives with each unique encounter.

In this example, we see the power of inclusion, even when instigated by a desperate sinner like me. However, inclusion is not the only strategy Jesus used to transform the conversation. We see by her response he's chosen the right visual aid too.

HANDY VISUAL AIDS

Today, water is still a precious commodity, the perfect comparison to both truth and eternal life. Not to mention, water is a lovely reflection of God's own Spirit. Unlike other treasured commodities, like gold and silver, water's special properties are life-giving. Picking up on her reference to Jacob's well, Jesus continued using his handy visual aid—water—to illustrate the abstract truth he poured out.

She needed a relationship with a Savior.

If only. If only my heart can trust him. If only what he says is true.

Her imagination stretched to consider his idea. Nothing triggers the imagination like a comparison of a physical item to an abstract idea. We can ponder analogies for days. Children love them. Visual aids are a formidable tool to get past others' objections and preconceived ideas, as we see here.

Anna's family celebrates a great example of visual aids when they light candles for Advent. Like water, candles have an abstract quality because light itself is transitory. Plus, children love the way candles flicker. I confess, I always thought of Advent wreaths as sort of ritualistic churchiness, so I never bothered to explore their purpose.

Not one to waste a perfectly delightful visual aid, my artist daughter and her husband allow their children to engage in "Jesus's birthday" in all the ways small children do. They read their favorite Christmas board books, sing silly songs, recite the story using plastic creche scenes, and blow out all the candles together.

Imagine my surprise when I heard my small grandchildren reciting a thousand details of the Christmas story and discovered they were lighting all four candles each and every night, sometimes in the bathtub. Like Jesus at the well, my daughter and her husband took something familiar, a candle, to teach beautiful truths to their children. They engage the children's imaginations with wonder and delight, tailoring their message for their own beloved children.

Whatever visual aid is handy is often the best one. In fact, even a bad analogy can make for a funny, yet still thought-provoking conversation. For instance, if you tell a small boy that any abstract idea reminds you of a stick or a ball, you'll have his undivided attention. Even if he informs you there's no way obedience or loyalty or courage is like a stick, does it matter? Just proving you are wrong means the child is totally engaged.

ENGAGING THE IMAGINATION OF CHILDREN AND GRANDCHILDREN

It's so easy to confuse opinion with truth in the world we inhabit. Social media is selling lies to our kiddos daily. My social media told me today I could lose weight if I'd just click on their app. It's a wonder any of us resist the temptation to follow such foolishness.

THE WELL

To build a life-long foundation for our children and grand-children, we need to seek diligently after the truth ourselves. With a little imagination, we can spark a child's interest in spiritual truths. In his book, *Pastor David's Travel Guide to Heaven*, David Dykes tells a story about how his mother introduced him to deeply spiritual truths about heaven.

> My mother was a devoted believer, but I remember she didn't have a lot of detailed answers. I'm sure she grew annoyed by my peppering her with questions while she was trying to finish the dishes. She finally smiled at me, took a deep breath, and just said, "David, Heaven is more wonderful than you can ever imagine." I went to bed that night intrigued. If Heaven was better than anything I could imagine, then that had to be something. I've always had a very active imagination that landed me in a lot of trouble when I was a young kid because I often got lost in the plot of the adventure books that I read under the covers by flashlight way after bedtime. There was no way I could sleep that night because I was too busy trying to picture what Heaven was like.[2]

I love the way his mother engaged his imagination to get him asking questions. I picture a boy under the covers with a flashlight, imagining how his long-term future could include an amazing place called heaven. What a clear example of how a mom's comment can spark her child's imagination.

Like the candles my daughter's family lights, Jesus is the light. Our imaginations can hardly fathom Jesus's presence in heaven, like Pastor David's example. God's Spirit is the living water, like the water drawn from Jacob's well. Jesus is the truth, quenching the thirst in our inner hearts. Of course, we long to share his Spirit and his truth with all those we love. Visual aids are one effective way to spark imagination and share truth.

Jesus Is the Truth

The best picture of real truth is Jesus. In John 14:6, Jesus says, "I am ... the truth." You can't get any more credible than that.

We are not Jesus, and, therefore, we're not exactly the embodiment of truth all the time. Maybe we embody truth for a moment on a good day. In contrast, Jesus is always the truth.

If it was productive for Jesus to engage others' imaginations, how much more necessary is it for us? In conversational adventures, we want others to see past their prejudices, past our frailties, and past our credentials or lack of them.

If only. If only I can put aside my insecurities and draw deeply from my heart.

Why not? Why not share authentically because I want others to see the truth of Jesus.

Imagination an Ongoing Tool for Inclusion

Without imagination, it's nearly impossible to be empathetic or compassionate. Without empathy or compassion, how can we truly love? Imagination is vital to all relationships.

We enhance our own imagination by allowing ourselves to question and challenge any cultural mythology we may have picked up along the way, even entrenched tradition. It's okay to reimagine old traditions, just like my daughter's family remade the tradition of the Advent candles.

We can set aside corrupted traditions or remake beautiful ones into fresh teaching tools. By fostering our own imagination, we equip ourselves to be more insightful and compassionate. In doing so, we give ourselves freedom to experience joy. With insight and compassion, we also discern the difference between opinion and truth.

Truth is a word that gets tossed around a lot. Personally, I struggle to slow down and ponder with wisdom. Imagining beyond our own experiences is a valuable skill to pass on to our children. For instance, one way to teach children compassion is to help them imagine how another person feels.

"How do you think Johnny felt today when the other kids were laughing at him," asks a wise mother of her young child.

A perfect example of failing to imagine beyond my experience happened in my first job. A lady I worked with daily seemed to dislike me. I kept wondering what I had done to offend her. My mind imagined a thousand small offenses, but she seemed too mature to trip over something trifling. Finally, as she was leaving for a new job, I got up the nerve to ask her if I had offended her. "Oh no," she answered in surprise. "It's your perfume. I'm allergic to it."

Until that moment, I never imagined she was holding her breath every time we met.

Fortunately, we don't have to be all-knowing when it comes to communication. We can ask perceptive questions and listen as the other person shares their objections and frustrations. We can open a conversation with God through prayer and wait patiently as we see answers unfold. Then, with a little imagination, we can keep conversational adventures rolling in a healthy direction.

WATERING THE IMAGINATION

Jesus tapped her imagination with seemingly hyperbolic promises. Imagine how his assurance of "will never thirst" must have caught her attention. Outlandish, certainly, but what could he possibly mean?

If only I didn't have to come here to this well every day in this searing heat.

He pushed past the obvious and caused her to consider the spiritual parallel of her physical reality.

"But the water that I shall give him will become in him a fountain of water springing up into everlasting life" (v. 14). In that bold assertion, Jesus targeted the most sacred place in her heart—her hope of everlasting life. Did she recognize her heart's desire instantly? Was she hoping to draw deeply and to know deeply?

If only. If only I could experience everlasting life.
What if? What if everlasting life could gush from my life?

Surely, the solitary woman who came to the well alone hoped for deep, authentic companionship. Like so many people in our modern age, perhaps every one of us, was she searching for more intimacy, more fellowship, and eternal meaning?

We know the end of this story recorded for us by witnesses. The living water he promised soon overflowed from her heart. In the same afternoon, she shared the same living water with her neighbors.

If only. If only everyone I know could meet the Savior.
Why not? Why not introduce them? He's right here at our well!
Oh, what joy!

Watering the imagination sometimes takes guts, especially when truth is at stake. However, like doctors at the hospital, diagnosing problems allows us to freely focus on solutions.

EARNING THE RIGHT TO BE HEARD

People sometimes persecute us for presenting an extraordinary idea. We may even come to believe we're required to be experts or authorities to deserve respect for our ideas. We hear phrases like, "You have to earn the right to be heard." Much like the question, "Who do you think you are?" this comment divides us into two groups, people who have earned the right to be heard and those who haven't.

In fact, people repeat the comment, "You have to earn the right to be heard," so often we may be fooled into believing it's true. Yet truth stands on its own merit, whether anyone thinks the person speaking deserves to be heard or not.

At times, we've all offered terrific insights that get us labeled. Labels can go in either extreme. We can be labeled as too negative or too impractical. Unfortunately, no matter how awesome your idea is, sometimes folks insist you must earn the right to be heard.

It may seem like they are challenging your credentials, but the reality may be entirely different. Sometimes they just want you to shut up and do it their way. Their reaction may be a silent confession about their lack of imagination. Even good leaders can become burned out. In contrast, healthy leadership will foster a vibrant exchange of ideas. Healthy leaders have earned the right to listen and they know it.

I sat at a table of women, united in our love of our community. As we giggled and passed around cell phone pictures of grandkids, a dear friend dashed over to hand me a glossy flyer. In whispered tones, she voiced her excitement. A happy-faced child in pigtails smiled up at me from the picture. Behind her stood a lemonade stand.

What if someone told that sweet child she was too young and inexperienced to make a difference in our world? Thank heaven no one told her she needed to earn the right to be heard. Or that her idea was too juvenile or too outlandish. Thank heaven my friend listened to this young lady and encouraged her dream, enlisting others to help too.

You better believe her vision inspired me. For the price of a Chick-Fil-A sandwich, I wrote a small check and handed it off to my friend to deliver. Within a few weeks, I received a personal thank you note from her in childish script reporting her tremendous success at her first—and definitely not last—fundraiser.

If only. If only we remembered the joy of unlimited possibility and lemonade stands.

What if? What if we encouraged all others to join the conversation, relishing a fresh perspective?

Like a child with a lemonade stand and a heart to serve, our imaginations allow us to love others with creative vigor. Imagination is not just about visual aids or finding ways to share truth at home or at work. God gave us imagination so we could find creative ways to integrate everything in our lives toward one goal. The purpose of our imagination is to live gently present, yet fiercely eternal with tender compassion for others.

IMAGINATION: A CRUCIAL ELEMENT IN LOVING GOD AND LOVING OTHERS

Jesus stayed true to his greater purpose to love God and love her. With imaginative genius, Jesus offered the woman at the well the thing she most craved in her heart. He offered her companionship with himself, comparing God's Spirit to living water. Plus, in a most beautiful double blessing, he nudged her imagination to consider how she might obtain this living water to share with others. This is the woman who came to the well alone. In obtaining living water, she enters rich companionship with her Savior and with her community.

For another terrific example of how clearly Jesus communicated about companionship, we go to an account in Matthew. A Pharisaic lawyer challenged Jesus to name the greatest of all the many (oh-so-many) commandments. By Jesus's time, there were so many extra commandments added to the original teachings this question was a little like trying to find one specific tree in a huge forest. Quick as a wink, though, Jesus reduced all commandments and all prophetic teaching to two simple principles.

> "Teacher, which *is* the great commandment in the law?" Jesus said to him, "You shall love the LORD your God with all your heart, with all your soul, and with all your mind." This is *the* first and great commandment. And *the* second *is* like it: "You shall love your neighbor as yourself." (Matthew 22:36–39)

Jesus reduced all Judeo/Christian teaching to two essential truths: Love God and love others. God exists, we don't make him up in our imaginations. But, when we love God or anyone else, our imaginations become a powerful tool. To love God, we must have faith to believe God exists and cares for us. To love others, we must have empathy and compassion. But how do we get empathy and compassion? By imagining the reality of the other person's experience.

Empathy is the ability to imagine how another person feels. Compassion requires us to imagine what would comfort another person. For instance, I never knew how important hugs could be at a funeral until my dad died. I lacked empathy because my imagination could not fathom how painful it is to lose a parent. Our own experiences with pain help us understand what another person may feel.

When we have grieved the loss of a loved one personally, we find it easier to imagine what kind of comfort might help someone else. Our pain produces compassion as we pass along comfort we received along the way. Now, I offer hugs with tender empathy at funerals. It's easy for me to imagine how much pain and mental fog a grieving person experiences. In sorrow and joy, imagination is vital to all relationships.

Without imagination, companionship and community would not exist. Jesus offers the woman at the well living water, but she must trust God's Spirit as the source of all companionship. She must imagine others will respond with joy, too. She imagined sharing the companionship offered by the Savior. Our imaginations become a crucial element in loving God and loving others.

The great Creator God gifted us with an amazing blessing when he created human imagination. Empathetic, compassionate communication magnifies relationships. Conversational adventures depend on imagination. Imagination, applied with compassion and wisdom, is our best hope of companionship and community.

When people challenge our credibility, about God's truth or anything else, we can relax. If we seek the truth, we will find it. Especially as Christians, because of Jesus, we can access truth through the Scriptures and through prayer. We are empowered by his Spirit. What a deep well from which to draw.

As we devote ourselves to imagining the perspective of others, we can choose inclusion, pick up the first handy visual aid we find—like a bucket of water or a wreath of candles—and keep sparking the imagination of those we hope to influence for pure good.

Focusing on Jesus's powerful strategies for claiming our influence means dreaming *If only* and asking *Why not?* For encouragement, keep this in mind: when folks start in with objections or challenge our credibility, we've probably already lit their imagination. They just can't picture it. Yet.

BEST QUESTION ABOUT IMAGINATION

What threatens your plans to have a difficult conversation?

The biggest threat to conversation is getting sidetracked by the irrelevant. We tend to take everything a little too personally, especially if we are naturally tenderhearted. That's why parents do their children a huge favor when they teach them to use their imagination about others' perspectives. Children who grow up learning to focus their conversations will be more successful in all aspects of life as adults.

We can teach our children a few simple questions to ask when engaged in conversational adventures. *Is there more to this story? What are the real needs of the person who's talking? What dreams and hopes can I help expedite for this person?*

Developing strong compassion muscles means we are prepared to respond with insight when others personally attack us. We can recognize the real need and respond with comfort and encouragement, rather than getting sidetracked.

Not only does your imagination equip you for authentic conversations; it also sparks imagination in others. No wonder Jesus used imagination with joy.

PRACTICAL TIP: PAIR OBJECTIONS WITH IMAGINATIVE VISION

As you consider a conversational adventure you would like to initiate, ask God to help you list all possible objections the other person may present. Try to imagine an inspiring future to match the real needs of the person you want to engage in conversation. It may help to write your list in two columns, pairing potential objections with powerful visual aids that ignite imagination.

For example, when our son was a young teenager, he was eager to be independent. He sometimes saw me as the enemy of his autonomy. I often said to him, "Son, no one is working harder for your independence than me. My biggest job as a mom is to help you become autonomous." Then, I helped him imagine what the next step in his path looked like, whether it was staying overnight at a friend's house or learning to drive the car. I was always surprised how well his imagination functioned when it came to his adult future.

What if, in your current situation, there's something to quench the real thirst, if only you can imagine it? Your imagination is your best gift, paired with prayer. Ask God to give you wisdom about the real needs of the person with whom you wish to talk.

As a leader and influencer, it's your responsibility to hear the perspective of others. When we are not in leadership, sometimes our only responsibility is to speak up. We also may need to wait patiently for others to imagine the possibilities. Jesus, the Master of Communication, also waited patiently for human imagination to catch up. What better way to ask for God's help in imagining the possibilities than prayer? For us, imagination and prayer go together.

MAY WE PRAY TOGETHER?

Dear Father in heaven, you are the one who created us to enjoy fellowship with you. Help us open our hearts and minds to imagine all the possibilities as we pray to you. Communication is one of your special gifts to us. All of us struggle to share ideas that may offer hope and vision. Often the people who need solutions most are the ones most determined to offer objections. Help us recognize real needs. Inspire us to think creatively, engaging the imagination of those we influence. Give us the questions we should be asking. Teach us to use our own imaginations with purity, grace, and self-discipline so our children can learn from us. Bless us now because that's your heart's desire. In Jesus's name. Amen.

"The true sign of intelligence is not knowledge but imagination."
—Albert Einstein

CHAPTER 6:

EVERYONE HAS A STORY

ARE WE DISQUALIFIED BECAUSE OF OUR PAST?
ABSOLUTELY NOT! THERE'S ALWAYS MORE TO THE STORY
AND IT MAY INVOLVE LIVING WATER.

> The woman said to Him, "Sir, give me this water,
> that I may not thirst, nor come here to draw." Jesus
> said to her, "Go, call your husband, and come here."
> (John 4:15–16)

Coaching other leaders to speak with clarity and zing is her special calling in life. She stood poised and triumphant before an audience of colleagues and delivered a compelling speech. She returned to her seat amid enthusiastic applause. "Boy, was that hard," she murmured.

Her speech was difficult to give because she'd made a courageous decision to share a personal story from her past about being raped. I've lost track of how many times I've witnessed a person share a personal story with trembling courage. They win the hearts of their audience by sharing with authenticity. There is power in vulnerability.

Communicating is hard for those who excel at it. What about the rest of us? Sometimes, we disqualify ourselves when we consider our own story. Perhaps our past seems too difficult to overcome, much less share—whether it's something we've done or something someone else did to us. The woman at the well set a dynamic example of courage and faith for us all.

She had the courage to tell Jesus the truth, rather than hide in shame. Plus, she trusted Jesus to respond with mercy and grace. In this part of the passage, we observe some of Jesus's strategies for confirming worth in surprising ways by

- recognizing her ready heart,
- acknowledging her past with compassion, and
- testing her grit.

READINESS QUALIFIES US

Readiness qualifies us. The past does not disqualify anyone. We all have something in our past we hesitate to share even with our closest friends. Obviously, we want to be careful who we trust with our most tender stories. When we drum up our courage and go for it, however, we may be surprised at the results.

One day at lunch with two dear friends, one friend shared the most scandalous thing she'd ever done. As she spoke, our other friend and I burst out laughing. Surprised and a little miffed, she asked, "What's so funny?" We both responded, "Is that really the worst thing you've ever done? Ours are so much worse!" Seriously, sometimes the only way to find out your past is not as bad as you thought is to share it with a trusted friend.

Was the woman at the well disqualified because of her reputation? No. No matter what we commonly assume about her reputation, past experience, or the legitimacy of her current relationships, Jesus devoted his undivided attention to her. Based on the way she ultimately influenced her whole community, she appears to have been able to relay the message.

What qualified her? There were scholars more educated than her. There were women with stable families. A whole batch of community leaders were nearby. Who was this woman who came to the well alone? Why did Jesus seek her out and devote his attention to her? The answer is simple—she was ready to hear.

"Give me this water," she said. By claiming his offer of living water, she stepped forward into the relationship with him. She began to recognize his status as Savior, *her* Savior. His message became hers.

Only Jesus Can Judge Rightly. The Rest of Us Can't.

As people of influence, we want to be sensitive to other people's experiences. However, we can't judge the whole story because most of the time we don't have it. As the story of the woman at the well proves, we don't need to know all the juicy details about her past. Obviously, if her past mattered so much, the New Testament writers would have given us more detailed information. Still, do you wonder about her past? I sure do.

Lives are nuanced experiences. Even when we think we know the facts, we are unqualified to judge. There is one righteous judge, and it isn't us. Besides, we all occasionally have trouble making sense of our own lives. I like what Ernest Kurtz and Katherine Ketcham wrote in *The Spirituality of Imperfection* about how our past stories can connect us with others.

"Rather than trying to tell their listeners' stories, rather than imposing interpretations, the sages and saints told the kind of stories that invited *identification*. They understood what the ancients had discovered: *The best way to help me find my story is to tell me your story.*" (italics in original)[1]

Sharing our own stories opens the door to finding those who are trustworthy and ready to hear. Readiness is an identifiable trait. As I've studied these verses about the woman at the well, I believe readiness alone qualifies us all to be people of influence.

Certainly, our past does not disqualify us. Plus, Jesus invites me to turn my story over to him, too, by showing compassion to this woman at the well. For that reason, I pay close attention to what the Savior said to this woman about her story.

The Problem with Tradition

Consider a question deserving a more thoughtful examination. Why do we assume the woman had a bad reputation?

I like what Liz Curtis Higgs said in her book, *It's Good to Be Queen*, about the Queen of Sheba. Liz also references Ruth and Mary Magdalene as other examples.

"I won't jump on my soapbox long, but I confess, I weary of scholars, interpreters, and commentators—male *and* female— reducing commendable women in Scripture to prostitutes, adulteresses, and mere objects of male desire ... Nothing in the original Hebrew or Greek or in any ancient historic records supports these myths."[2] Thank you, Liz, for speaking up with scholarly confidence.

Can we please add the woman at the well to our list of misunderstood women? I have a problem with the standard depiction of the woman at the well. Like a detective in a TV drama, I say, "Something about the story seems off to me."

We owe it to ourselves to think more thoroughly about what could be at play in this account. Why? Being compassionate about the woman at the well prepares us for the real work of connecting with real people in our own lives. There's always more to anyone's story. Rather than judging, condemning, and dismissing the woman at the well with the label promiscuous, let's consider a few other possibilities.

Jesus says, "the one whom you now have is not *your* husband" (John 4:18b, italics mine). Jesus is exposing sin.

Clearly, the woman and "her" man are not married. Certainly, the longer we meditate on the words of Jesus here one thing becomes crystal clear. He is offering this woman forgiveness for herself and others, plus freedom. Oh, if only we could remember to offer such compassion to those who suffer, no matter the toll sin takes on their lives!

In a startling conversational pivot, Jesus starts to count her husbands, as we will examine more thoroughly in the next chapter. He says, "For you have had five husbands, and the one whom you now have is not your husband; in that you spoke truly" (John 4:18).

Jesus told her to go get her ανηρ or *aner,* a word commonly used to indicate husband. Yet, we discover in the next few comments Jesus knew she was not married.

Was Jesus tricking her? Never. Was he testing her? Maybe. He may have been giving her a chance to acknowledge the truth about her situation. When she states she has no husband, did she confess her own sin? Maybe. It's likely Jesus is offering her a chance to tell the truth about her life.

Whether her station in life came as a result of her own sin or the sin of others or just the natural flow of life, we don't know. Perhaps some combination of events explains the number of her husbands. Was she abandoned along the way? Abused? Adulterous? Immoral? Divorced? Widowed? Maybe widowed more than once? Or some combination of all. We simply don't know.

Jesus points out the painful truth, of any sin or heart-break with compassion, not the condemnation she may have received from others. We'll have to wait for heaven to hear her whole story, but in the meantime, we can learn a lot from the respectful way Jesus handled the details of her life, which he undoubtedly understood thoroughly.

MORE TO THE STORY

My main goal here is to clarify one essential truth on behalf of all women. We owe it to ourselves to think through the way Jesus interacted with people, especially with women. Since we often lack the information we need, our best bet is to interact with empathy to the best of our ability. There was obviously much more to this woman's story.

Jesus does not skip the truth to make the woman feel more comfortable. He shows mercy and understanding in spite of the sin reflected in her experience. By giving her a chance to own her current situation, Jesus leads her to the "living water." He is inviting her into a life rich in forgiveness and grace, a life of companionship, joy, and influence.

As one friend suggested to me, Jesus tended "to speak to the outcast in society." As modern readers, we notice his ability to love universally, without regard to society's mandates. Perhaps the uniting factor in all Jesus's interactions, no matter the person's status in society or gender or their background, was the readiness of the other person's heart to receive his message.

It's easy for women to serve everyone else and still feel invisible. This is a common feeling modern people often experience. Maybe our imagination best serves us by trying to understand all the various challenges women faced then and still face today.

New Testament writers omit so much detail about the woman's story. I honestly don't care what her past included. My point is simple. We need to push pause before we jump to conclusions and condemn people. We are invited by tradition to make many assumptions about this woman's moral status. I invite you to pursue solid information, rather than buying into the preconceived notion of anyone's past. Certainly, we are better off when we ask gentle questions and trust God with other peoples' stories.

While speculating about the woman's untold story may be fascinating, we really don't have enough information to draw hard and fast conclusions. I am comforted when I notice the way Jesus did not let her past or untold story disqualify her at all. Instead, her ready heart opened a new story in her life, one of influence and community. Her social status is unclear to us. Yet, Jesus chose her because she was ready and waiting for him.

As we read the passage of Jesus's encounter with the woman at the well in particular, we get a better idea of the compassion Jesus is lavishing on this woman. In fact, his compassion and understanding can inform our responses to people's stories even now, thousands of years later.

ACKNOWLEDGING THE PAST WITH COMPASSION

As a writer and podcaster, I hear folks' stories all the time. Yet, even in our open society, people are reticent to share their most intimate stories for fear of retribution about past sin—theirs or another person's sin. Often there is excruciating pain associated with past experiences. Obviously, it's considered rude to ask intrusive questions. Even someone as trusted as a pastor may not hear the full story.

Jesus referenced the woman at the well's past without shaming her, when he said, "Go, call your husband, and come here." He simply told the truth—"the one whom you now have is not your husband"—and he did so with compassion. Using this conversation technique can be one way to free people from their past. Like Jesus, when people share their heartbreak with us, we must listen with compassion and not condemnation.

The woman at the well clearly had traumatic experiences in her past. Letting go of the past becomes essential for all of us who have painful stories. It's not about pretending something didn't happen, but about freedom. In her book, *Deal With It!*, Paula White writes about pressing on to the future, while letting the past inform us without binding us.

> I had to make the decision to "forget" the things behind. Forgetting does not mean that I developed amnesia. I still have a memory about tragic events I've experienced. But ... I chose not to dwell on those memories. I choose not to rethink those same sickening thoughts that once led me to depression. I choose not to think about the times when I was locked in a closet as a child. God's Word tells us, "As he thinks in his heart, so is he" (Prov. 23:7). Our thoughts become our words. Our words become our actions. Our actions become our habits. Our habits become our character. And our character becomes our destiny. You must *choose* to forget and leave the past behind.[3]

In addition, people often share a common experience of grieving over some loss associated with relationships. For instance, when a child dies before a parent, the parent often has many regrets about lost opportunities in the relationship. Regret further compounds grief in relationships strained due to sin. Many relationships spin out of control quickly, marked by habitual arguing, anger, addiction, and many other destructive choices. Some losses are obvious. Some are extremely private.

THE COMFORT OF TRUTHFUL INSIGHT

Jesus's tenderness toward the woman at the well is all the more powerful, knowing how complicated relationships can be. Perhaps she felt comforted by his insight about her past. How her heart must have responded to the truth Jesus offered here. He offers her—and us—a fresh perspective of freedom and accountability. Not only do we reevaluate our feelings about her past, but our own past as well.

Like the woman at the well, a truthful assessment of our past can be freeing.

With Jesus's unconditional love, forgiveness, and affirmation, she chose freedom from her past by acknowledging it to Jesus. Like the woman at the well, we are free to offer true love, forgiveness, affirmation, and compassion to others.

TESTED GRIT

Whatever her story, Jesus brilliantly tests her grit. His initial remark to go get her current husband could have easily wilted her. In asking her this, he is giving her an opportunity to display the depth of her courage and willingness to embrace the truth.

Would she desire a relationship with him enough to get past his factual question about her painful circumstances? He exposes her deep desire to know the Savior. She comes through with brilliant clarity. She had to deal truthfully with him to move on. To help her, he offered her something she could hardly resist: inclusion and never thirsting again.

Living water? Were there other possibilities she'd never considered? What exactly is he offering? We get a hint to the answers to these questions in John 7. Ironically, it's the Pharisees who again prompt this beautiful description of God's Spirit.

> On the last day, that great *day* of the feast, Jesus stood and cried out, saying, "If anyone thirsts, let him come to Me and drink. He who believes in Me, as the Scripture has said, out of his heart will flow rivers of living water." But this He spoke concerning the Spirit, whom those believing in Him would receive. (John 7:37–39)

Like so many people today, the woman at the well needed emotional and spiritual energy, and she knew it. Jesus knew it too. His message still sparks dreams in our hearts when we understand what he really offers. Jesus presents a relationship with God's Spirit, a true connection with himself.

She opened herself up to a whole new way of living and thinking as she connected with his message. God's own Spirit is a tremendous source of energy and joy. Soon, his Spirit will flow out of her heart like rivers of water.

What a promise! To receive it, she must step up and claim it. "The woman said to Him, 'Sir, give me this water, that I may not thirst, nor come here to draw'" (John 4:15). She dares to claim what he offers.

Jesus clearly communicates he knows her story as she begins to understand what she wants. How tempting it can be to short-cut truth. We make it too easy on folks, I suspect. We want to prejudge people without giving them a chance to show their readiness or their courage.

We instinctively skip the part of the process where we ask people the hard questions. When we do, we cheat ourselves out of a chance to love folks unconditionally and to be so loved ourselves.

ASK THE HARD QUESTIONS

One example of how appealing it can be to skip a hard question came years ago in Louisiana. Living in a new place as a young couple, David and I were thrilled to get to know another couple. One night over dinner, the husband began to tell us story after astonishing story, like something out of an action movie. Hallucinations or dreams or paranoia? His stories sounded too crazy to be true.

Skeptical, I hated to say out loud my suspicion that some of the details had been fabricated. *Could he seriously think we'd believe these far-fetched stories actually happened to him?* I began to pray for understanding about what was going on. Finally, I felt God's Spirit nudge me to ask an unexpected question. Feeling foolish, I said, "This may sound silly, I guess, but have you ever considered suicide?"

My husband sat rigidly next to me. His smile, only moments ago tender, became a thin line. I could feel David's dismay and I dared not look his way. Then, amazingly, the husband answered with a whispered, "How did you know?"

"I had no idea myself," I said, "but I was willing to take a chance because I thought I recognized God's quiet Spirit in my heart prodding me." This, I believe, conveyed God's concern for this couple. With relief, he and his wife began to share the struggles they were facing because of his growing depression and mental confusion. Thankfully, they had good medical care. There was very little help we could offer, except to care about them without judgment or rejection.

Like Jesus, we simply must learn to ask the hard questions. Conversational adventure includes disciplining ourselves to handle the truth about people's experience with tenderness and compassion. In doing so, we open opportunity for comfort and new understanding. By accepting people's most intimate stories without condemnation, we affirm the value inherent in each person, including ourselves.

Another example of how dealing truthfully qualifies us and proves our resilience is in the stories being told publicly throughout the US now when it comes to abortion. For so many years, women like me who'd experienced abortion were too ashamed to talk openly. In fact, post-abortion syndrome (PAS) is so common, it's recognized as a condition similar to post-traumatic stress disorder (PTSD).

I hid my abortion for years until finally my secret robbed me of all joy. When I ran out of emotional energy to hide, I sought help and began sharing my story with close friends. Their loving, unconditional support helped heal my heart. Years later, when I felt called to speak about my experience in public, I realized I had another batch of lingering shame to examine. I was able to step into the life and writing career God prepared for me by trusting Jesus's sacrifice on the cross to be enough for me.

Believe me when I say, truth can test our grit. It's an ongoing act of faith each time I share the stories of my life, reflecting the sacredness of God's forgiveness and grace extended to me. Each time I tell the truth about how little I deserve his mercy and love, I honor his gift to me. In doing so, I acknowledge that he sees me as priceless, worthy, and significant. We must draw deeply from the well of his unfailing love to trust him. That takes courage and grit.

We see any experiences in our past washed and purified by his grace when we turn them over to Jesus. His Spirit is truly like living water, washing our hearts and minds clean.

Jesus knows and compassionately understands every sorrow we hide away in our hearts. He seeks us out and waits for us at the well of his love. Like the woman at the well, we must be willing to imagine a different future for ourselves. I hope you, too, will imagine a world where we all claim the pure influence God wants to bestow on each of us.

Culture Shift

Nowhere is grit more tested than in our current culture. We watch the nightly news often feeling dismay as our leaders and elected officials bicker like spoiled children. It seems we can't have a civil conversation in our culture now. What if polarized and dogmatic rhetoric is a symptom of disengaging our imaginations? Could it be we've forgotten how to discipline our minds to find the perfect analogies and words to convey truth in a gentle manner?

We may never be able to change what the folks on the nightly news say. Yet we can look to Jesus for strategies we can use in our own homes. Jesus recognized the readiness of the woman at the well and responded with truth. The truth he presented could easily shut down their conversation. To keep the conversation open, he presented more imaginative offers. Always, he stayed true to his goal of inviting her into eternal life and companionship with him. Those strategies can certainly create a shift in our homes. But wait. There's more.

Honestly, we just crave better conversations in our homes, no matter what happens to the culture at large. We may think instigating a culture shift is too big a task for little ole common folks like us, but what if it's not?

Like the woman at the well, Ruth was an outsider, a foreigner, in fact. The Bible tells us, in her tested devotion to Naomi, she found the love of her life, Boaz. She became an ancestor of Jesus himself. Consider what Paula White writes about Ruth and all the people in the Bible God used to create change.

> Every time God desires to change a nation, he sends a person who has been changed. That certainly was the case in Ruth's life. God changed her, and she changed history. You have the capability of ushering in a new season into the world. You carry within you the seed of a new season ... a new revival ... a new move by God. But to usher in that new season, you must leave the old.[4]

A culture changes with one person, one family, one community at a time. What if, by fostering imagination in our own minds and the minds of our kids, we could change the conversation in a whole culture? To do so, we must let go of the old things holding us back and claim what God is offering. A changed culture is possible especially if we join in prayer and ask God for a renewal of his living water. That's a worthy goal if I ever heard one.

Best of all, we don't do it alone. God raises up people, wherever they are ready. For example, I was privileged to attend the Christian Communicators Conference, an elite training program hosted by very talented ladies. There, I met women from all over the United States who are trained in multiple ways to present the message God has given them. Each of them influences their own communities and beyond.

Imagine the relief I felt to know I am not alone in grieving for our culture, where it seems fear is peddled with vigor in the media daily. In some states, fellow Christians tell me they are persecuted for their faith. More and more it seems folks perceive claiming the Christian faith as bold and counter-cultural, even downright crazy. Folks often respond with hostility these days when they discover we follow Christ. Now, as I sit at my desk, wrapping up the final draft of this book, I'm encouraged to press on because I know there are many voices offering hope to those who hurt throughout our culture.

Finally, Jesus enjoys her ardent response, having done his difficult and patience-testing work of creating an authentic conversation with the woman. With determination, she asks for the very thing he wants to give her. Now, we arrive at the culmination of a life-changing conversational adventure.

REFRESHING WATER FOR OUR SOULS

Living water is a wonderful word picture of how God's Spirit flows through our hearts. We can also picture God's Spirit by seeing how Jesus himself is described in the Bible. If reading and studying the Bible seems challenging, may I suggest a red-letter edition of the Bible? Focus on the things Jesus said, which are printed in red ink, thus the name. Of all the ideas in this book, this is my favorite suggestion. Red-letter Bibles are so awesome.

With a red-letter Bible, you can skim through all the words Jesus said in a very short time, maybe an hour or less. Then, whatever catches your imagination, spend time in that spot. Check out the context of why he said what he did.

May I encourage you to write notes to yourself or even doodle in the margins of your Bible? In case you feel weird writing in the Bible, let me assure you folks do it all the time, especially forgetful people like me. Some people even draw beautiful illustrations based on the words they read. From ancient times, this technique of doodling and creating art in the margins of a book was called illuminating. Today, museums display treasured illuminated Bibles from the Middle Ages.

Who knows? Maybe the Bible you study will be a cherished addition to someone's library long after you're gone. Many people also use a journal to keep a record of the things they discover about God.

What a good God who invites us to know him and be known. Certainly, our lives can be illuminated by him, over-flowing with the living water of his Spirit. My prayer is that you will get to know him in a richer and deeper way each day.

With the promise of living water, Jesus invited the woman from the physical realm to the supremely spiritual. This same promise is available to us if we can only imagine the possibilities. What a beautiful reward for our readiness and courage. We, too, can experience the living water of his Holy Spirit, flooding our lives and gushing out to soak others in love and joy.

Yes, indeed, there are more adventures to come.

BEST QUESTION ABOUT OUR PAST AND OUR STORIES

Keeping your past in mind, how would you describe God's Holy Spirit?

Our stories can begin to inform the way we think about God. Our past does not prevent God from loving us unconditionally. We hold intrinsic value to him. The past is not who we are or even who we once were. It's certainly not the end of our story. In my life, God is the One who forgives, the One who sets my feet on solid ground, who teaches me to guard my heart and mind, listens to my prayers, understands my groanings, heals my broken-hearted places, meets me in the inner sanctuary, champions the causes of those I love. Ah, I could go on and on.

Great news, God is not confused about you, your experiences, or your past. In Jesus, we have an invitation to get to know the God of the universe, just like the woman at the well did. We are invited into a relationship where we are fully known and loved.

In him, we have an exact portrait of God. Jesus is the message God wants us to have about himself. That's why Jesus is called *Logos*, translated the *Word*, in the opening verses of the book of John. Jesus is God's message to us, so we can understand what the God of the universe is actually like.

Likewise, his Spirit is exactly who God is too. As hard as it would be for us to imagine God otherwise, Jesus came to Earth and let his disciples touch, see, and hear him (1 John 1). He conversed with people, like the woman at the well. The disciples wrote about him so we could be filled with the same joy. God wants us to know all about him. Why? He wants us to have a relationship with him. He wants us for his companions, now and forever. He seeks us out, our past, our story, and all.

Just as your spirit is key to who you are, so we must understand God's Spirit to know him and who he is. That sounds complicated, but really, it's pretty easy. To imagine God's

Spirit, all we must do is describe Jesus. He is his Spirit. Getting to know him is so simple and clear.

PRACTICAL TIP: IMAGINE THE POSSIBILITIES

Tonight, take ten minutes to write down a vision you want for your future. Dream big. Include lots of details. Remember, God is in your favor. He knows your story and wants freedom and joy for you. You are his beautiful child, designed by him for pure influence in this messy world. He believes in you and wants to bless you. Consider what could happen if the living water of his Holy Spirit came flowing out of your heart to splash on everyone around you. What refreshing love!

What if the vision of your beautiful future included getting to know God as he truly is? How could you describe his Spirit? I have no idea what kind of personal blessings God is waiting to bestow on you, but I am confident of one thing. Like the woman at the well, we must ask God for what we want. We must be ready to receive what he offers. Stepping into our future requires grit. His Spirit wants to refresh you like a cool splash of water.

We all crave joy. Sometimes, though, we trip over our own stories. Thankfully, the past may not be quite as important as we think. Readiness is enough to qualify us. With truth comes freedom. With freedom comes joy.

We experience joy once in a while, and we can't get enough. Joy pops up in our lives and all around us when people smile and laugh. Like water, God's Spirit washes over us, and we rejoice. Oh, to be constant purveyors of living water and his joy.

MAY WE PRAY TOGETHER?

Dear Father in heaven, you refresh us with living water, so we thirst no more. Your beautiful Holy Spirit drenches us in love for others. Yet, here we are again, your grubby children. We still get bent out of shape. We fail to imagine other people's stories with empathy and compassion. How can we comfort others if we don't imagine their pain? Like small children, we keep running back to you to comfort our daily scrapes and bruises. We need you. We look to you now for the beauty of your Spirit. Fill our hearts with the love that flows out of you like water from a spring. Please drench us in your Spirit, we pray. May we understand the truth about who you are. Bless us now because that's your heart's desire. In Jesus's name. Amen.

My story is a freedom song of struggle. It is about finding one's purpose, how to overcome fear and to stand up for causes bigger than one's self.—Coretta Scott King

CHAPTER 7:
MAKE FACTUAL ASSESSMENTS

HOW CAN WE SPEAK THE TRUTH SO WE ARE HEARD?
FACTUALLY, WITHOUT REJECTION OR CONDEMNATION.

> The woman answered and said, "I have no husband."
> Jesus said to her, "You have well said, 'I have no
> husband,' for you have had five husbands, and the
> one whom you now have is not your husband; in
> that you spoke truly." (John 4:17–18)

In Texas, they say high school football is king. Yet, football teams can be tricky. I witnessed a great example of astute, factual assessment one day because of one young man's courage. The exchange happened in a high school locker room after the team was gone for the day.

I'm not an expert on sports, but apparently hazing is an accepted practice within some athletic circles. There seems to be a pecking order of authority, something about toughening up the younger players by letting the seniors pick on them.

The coach offered objections even as he tried to listen to the young man's perspective. With utmost confidence, the young man ignored the coach's objections and patiently explained why hazing was not appropriate even on football teams. He concluded the conversation with a gentle truth spoken in deep conviction.

"Yes, sir, but lording it over others is not true leadership."

I marveled as he held his coach accountable with this one honest fact. My heart went out to the coach, an excellent leader with a problem on his team. This student's factual assessment placed the coach in the awkward spot of correcting his key student leaders while maintaining discipline among the younger players. Meanwhile, all over Texas, coaches are under tremendous pressure to win games in order to keep their jobs. I bet the coach wished he'd never been held accountable by that conversationally adventurous young player.

We'll see how truth-telling with compassion can super-qualify us for influence. To prepare ourselves for pure influence, we'll examine how Jesus masterfully ushered the woman's heart to a place where she could embrace truth, by

- telling her the truth without rejection,
- rewarding her truthful assessment of her life with compassion, and
- taking the sting out of her past by accepting her.

TELLING THE TRUTH WITHOUT REJECTION

Our stories are often loaded with baggage. Therefore, it pays to look closely at how we can learn to diffuse baggage-induced bondage. How do we forgive others and move on? How do we forgive ourselves? It's not easy, but Jesus offers us some strategies about how to use honesty without rejection or condemnation. The trick is to assess our own life and heart factually before we start shoveling up facts for other people. When we embrace our own frailties, we also free ourselves to embrace others wholeheartedly.

Jesus's manner with the woman at the well bears a closer look. Let's review the scene at the well.

She asks a tough question, testing him. Jesus listens patiently without argument as she presents objections, including politically loaded issues and a challenge to his credentials. He responds with gentleness and creativity. *We wonder what she must have thought about him. Living water? This guy's kinda funny.* Who knows? But, certainly, he passes the first round of her tests.

Next, he tests her grit by requesting she go get her husband. She proves her commitment by responding with her own truth.

There's something about this stranger. With a look and a smile, he affirms her truthfulness. "You have well said, 'I have no husband.'"

Then, bam! He starts talking about her personal life, numbering her husbands. Really? She already said she wanted living water. I don't know about you, but my heart demands an explanation. Was he picking on her about how many times she'd been married? Why is he digging up the details, like an accountant in tax season?

We know her past did not disqualify her because we know the end of the story. What was he thinking? If she met the key qualification—readiness to hear—why bother to go over all the factual and embarrassing numbers? To answer that question, we must remember Jesus always dealt compassionately with everyone in their deepest needs.

If we assume Jesus was condemning her or holding her accountable for her past by numbering all the embarrassing details, we may misjudge the situation. Obviously, he knew all the nitty-gritty details already. He understood any false assumptions her neighbors may have harbored. What if, by recounting her story in a factual way, he took the sting out of it for her? What if, by doing so, he freed her from guilt and shame by giving her a chance to receive his complete, unconditional forgiveness and love? He doesn't care about her past. He cares about *her.*

Jesus communicates his acceptance of her—including her past—by addressing it directly. She has no more reason to cringe when others reject her because the Savior accepts her. She could freely move forward in confidence, in his love and acceptance. He frees her up to accept him as her Savior and friend by accepting her first. In summary, she could be confident because he knew and cherished her. Every stinking detail.

FINE FOR JESUS, BUT WHAT ABOUT ME?

Sure, we all know Jesus tells the truth with kindness and with a tender look in his eyes. But what about us? When it comes to loving people unconditionally to their core, I'm not Jesus. For me, keeping a tender look in my eyes can be murder, especially when I'm looking at someone I love who has hurt me, yet again. I'm pretty sure that person sees fury in my face. Ouch.

We better dig in and talk about the etiquette of truth-telling when two sinners are involved. Truth-telling is an important part of conversational adventures. We must draw deeply from the well of living water.

The most serious conversations in our lives often boil down to someone wanting to tell truth to someone who doesn't want to hear it. To do this well, we need to know how Jesus told the truth and why. From there, we can learn to be much more effective when difficult situations require a factual assessment. We especially need to walk in freedom rather than condemnation.

The United States has a long history of etiquette and civility, much of it established by our first president. I like the way George Washington refused to be turned into a king. This good man made a list of 110 rules for his own edification, recorded for us in a modern translation with notes by Ross Bolton. In fact, I bought this little jewel of a book for each of my grandsons, so they could read firsthand what our first president thought was proper in "company and communication." As an example, here's Rule #41:

"41. Undertake not to Teach your equal in the art himself Professes; it Savors of arrogancy. {Modern Translation: Don't teach those of similar status what they already know, to do so is arrogant.}"[1]

In his commentary, Bolton noted the biblical principle, "Matthew 7:4 states 'How can you say to your brother, "Let me take the speck out of your eye," when there is a plank in your own eye?'"[2]

The idea here is how can we possibly judge others when we are so often at fault ourselves? That's the problem with seeking the truth and telling it: truth has a way of finding us too. We want to tell the truth, but we don't necessarily want to hear it.

"I'm not judging you; I'm just telling you the truth." We've probably all heard that phrase and cringed, especially if it was directed at us. I confess, I used to say stuff like that all the time back when I was a lot younger. Now I know I've earned the right to stop talking and listen. But my goodness, sometimes truth is so hard to hear.

Our mouths seem to be the first way we go haywire. How do we speak truth factually and with compassion? When we consider how hard it is to keep our tongues under the rein of God's Spirit, it's a wonder we ever have any decent conversations at all.

We assume there was something in Jesus's manner that reassured the woman at the well because she continued to engage with him. Was it his tone of voice? His body language? Did he reach out with a warm gesture? Was it the look in his eyes? As he spoke the truth to her, perhaps, all those things conveyed his unconditional love, without rejection or condemnation.

OUT OF THE HEART, THE MOUTH SPEAKS

Our mouths naturally say all manner of embarrassing, selfish stuff. When they do, it's time to look deeper. Thoughts originate in the heart. Then our mouth gets to blabbing, like a squeaking windmill on a blustery day. To speak truth with compassion, we must set our heart right first. Our hearts can be rotten to the core or they can be places of good fruit and beautiful treasure.

Naturally, Jesus addressed our human capacity to say all the wrong things. He responded to our old friends, the Pharisees, on this very topic. In fact, he went so far as to call them a brood of vipers because their thoughts were so opposite of God's truth.

> Either make the tree good and its fruit good, or else make the tree bad and its fruit bad; for a tree is known by its fruit. Brood of vipers! How can you, being evil, speak good things? *For out of the abundance of the heart the mouth speaks.* A good man out of the good treasure of his heart brings forth good things, and an evil man out of the evil

treasure brings forth evil things. (Matthew 12:33–37, italics mine)

We would probably not be so bold as to call someone else a snake, especially since we're supposed to be good Christians and all. In this case, though, Jesus is using strong language to appeal to religious folks who have chosen to harden their hearts. He went straight to the heart of the problem—our hearts. The ideas we cherish and espouse are treasured in our hearts first.

It's safe to note Jesus took extreme measures because religiosity sounded a serious alarm in his soul. The Pharisees chose a dogmatic, man-made religiosity rather than the sacrificial, responsive spirituality Jesus lived and taught.

I used to read Jesus's words here as if loaded with condemnation. It took me years to realize he is offering the Pharisees a strong entreaty, with their best interests at its core. We can safely assume Jesus's motivation, although demonstrated to the Pharisees in harsh words, is the desire to redeem people and offer them a relationship with himself. He beautifully demonstrates this truth in action on the cross, where he died for anyone ready to receive him, including the Pharisees.

Unlike Jesus, we'd be embarrassed to claim name-calling is in folks' best interests. It's worth noting, however, Jesus dealt with religious hypocrisy sternly, even harshly. In contrast, he dealt tenderly and patiently with moral or social hypocrisy. In our own homes, his example can inform the way we engage in conversational adventures with our spouse, children, or extended family.

JUST TWO SINNERS TRYING TO TALK

Since this common problem of how sinners talk to each other is as old as dirt, we can dig back in history to one of the best collections of wise sayings ever written. The Book of Proverbs, included in the Old Testament, was written sometime before 500 B.C.[3]

Here we find classic principles to help us rein in our own tongues, while also teaching our kids and grandkids to communicate with compassion. First, speaking what is right is its own joy. Additionally, there's bonus joy in having the next generations adopt a habit of speaking what is right.

Proverbs 23:15–16 says, "My son, if your heart is wise my own heart also will be glad and my innermost being will rejoice when your lips speak what is right." Have you ever experienced the hollow feeling that your best work is wasted on your job? Here's a sure way to restore your sense of purpose and joy. Re-prioritizing what we think and talk about is an easy beginning, especially knowing future generations will benefit.

We can adopt wisdom as our ambition. Then work to pass it on as an inheritance to our children and grandchildren. The natural result of such effort will be beautiful fruit indeed, as our children freely speak about what is right.

Obviously, what is right is not what is self-righteous. Instead, a wise heart will nurture truth with tenderness and humility. For some of us, learning to speak out of a tender heart will take a lifetime.

As a doctor, my dad helped countless people in his practice of medicine. Along the way, he also developed a habit of unwinding with buddies over a glass of bourbon.

One day, a few other physicians invited him to come to their Alcoholics Anonymous meeting. Relieved to find people who understood his pain, he practiced sobriety one day at a time for the last thirty years of his life.

Rather than sitting back on his accomplishments as a physician, seeking humility became his ambition in his sobriety. Slowly, he began to share the traumatizing experiences he suffered while his dad was away during World War II. He began to share his story frequently, inviting many others to finish each day sober. Never one to judge and condemn others, he learned to rest in compassion for himself as well. As his own heart healed, he became an inspiring example of how a wise heart speaks truth to others with compassion and humility.

Next, as we see in Jesus's example with the Pharisees, a bold response can also be the most loving one. Proverbs 10:10 tells us, "People who wink at wrong cause trouble, but a bold reproof promotes peace." Teaching our children and grand-children when to speak what is right may mean standing up alone at times.

Whenever a youngster speaks up to stop bullying in a classroom, we see an excellent example of a bold reproof. Or when a young man speaks up to those in authority like the young player spoke up to his coach. Our kids must see us stand alone when necessary in order to have the courage to speak up when others don't.

Do we wink at racist jokes or justify certain habits by labeling them only minor sexual innuendos? Are we willing to ask the right questions to hold ourselves and others account-able? Does the dread of push back keep us from speaking up at church or at work? Yes, of course, we've all experienced these or similar situations. But courage and humility are our armor as we claim the pure influence God intends for us to have.

The idea of promoting peace with a bold reproof applies especially well when it comes to boundaries. At home or at work, there are times when telling the truth is the best strategy for promoting and preserving peaceful relationships. Yet, we often find ourselves defending new boundaries whenever we try to establish them. In those moments, a peaceful environ-ment is established as we boldly state our factual desire to keep the new boundary in place.

For instance, since we had the first grandbaby on both sides of the family, David and I did a ton of boundary setting at first. One time, I put down some new boundaries with my dad, and he pushed back. Always a great communicator himself, he reminded me of the many times we crossed pastures in my youth, climbing through barbed wired fences to hunt.

"I feel like you're putting up 'No Trespassing' signs," Dad complained. His challenge to my parenting decision bugged me. I explained the new boundary one more time and said goodbye.

"People put up 'No Trespassing' signs because people trespass," remarked David.

Thank you!

Eventually, all the grandparents grew to respect the thought-ful care we put into raising our kids. Our bold reproof—setting clear boundaries about what we expected from the new grand-parents—developed into peaceful, harmonious relationships.

Finally, thinking about good communication etiquette, we want to be on guard against quarrelsomeness. Proverbs 20:3 warns, "It is honorable for a man to stop striving, since any fool can start a quarrel." Have you noticed, in our debate-infatuated society, we seem to argue a lot?

As a naturally talkative person, with a philosophical bent, I realized I was guilty of trying to convince people of my opinion by repeating myself. As if repetition ever persuaded anyone of anything.

I still struggle to speak tenderly rather than bluntly. Therefore, I developed a couple of simple clues to keep myself honest on this score. I could call them rules, I guess, but rules sound burdensome. Giving myself a clue means no one else is expected to live by my "rules." I'm pretty sure my family prefers it this way. Here are my self-informing clues to avoid arguments.

DON'T BE ARGUMENTATIVE

We must discipline our heart to resist arguing. I wish I could claim I was smart enough to figure this out without needing these clues myself. Sadly, the opposite is true. I guess I could pretend to be perfect here, but too many of my friends know better. So, here they are—Cathy's clues for avoiding quarrels.

Clue #1—Share my opinion once. The first time I share something, I'm simply offering my opinion.

Clue #2—Let the other person have an opinion too. The other person is free to respect my opinion, consider it, reject it, or *ick*, even mock it. They may bluntly tell me I'm wrong. And yep, that's even if I'm convinced I'm right.

Clue #3—Never repeat in the face of objections. It's oh-so-tempting to repeat the same opinion over and over, in hopes the other person will hear your valid point. In my experience, though, repetition never persuades. Therefore, if I repeat my opinion, I consider my behavior argumentative.

"How do I get my point across to my husband if I can't repeat myself?" I asked my friend in frustration. I sought her wisdom, but I didn't like her answer one bit. She explained how I could wait and reintroduce important topics in different ways later, thus avoiding an argument. Somehow this went against all my instincts. But truthfully, I knew repetition was not gaining ground with my rational, linear-thinking husband. Communication between two people wired so differently required creativity and patience.

My husband always takes the time he needs to consider all possible consequences of significant decisions. My natural responsiveness and instinctive decisiveness bewilder him.

Taking her advice, I noticed a trend. I successfully triggered his imagination best when I approached difficult topics with a step-by-step rationale. Now, when we disagree and before I try to explain my perspective, I pause, pray, ponder, and then proceed. Rather than argue, I try a different approach, or I return to the topic at another time.

If you find yourself repeating the same arguments, two truths jump out. First, the topic is important to you. Second, you may need a different approach. We all need multiple creative ideas about how to communicate truth, so conversations don't morph into arguments.

Now, you wouldn't think there's any silver lining to my problem. Obviously, it's painful to confess how much I've personally struggled with argumentativeness. But guess what? There's great news with this. Once I quit demanding a second and third re-statement of my opinion, I started noticing when other folks were argumentative.

What's even more interesting from my point of view is how many people stop with stating their opinion only once. Many, many polite folks state their opinion without arguing or telling you your opinion is wrong. In fact, they habitually listen with empathy and compassion. We probably won't see them on the nightly news, but I still think they're onto something powerful.

More interesting still, as I began practicing my clues for avoiding arguments, I noticed why people feel compelled to argue. Sometimes, they want to feel connected by being in any conversation, even an argument. Perhaps their conscience compels them to explain some truth they feel you're missing.

Maybe they don't know they're arguing. They want to help you understand their perspective, but they don't know how to use influence effectively.

Arguing can be motivated by the need for companionship since communication is the basis for all relationship building. Habitual arguing is symptomatic of immaturity. It designates a need for disciplined thinking and a commitment to use imagination to communicate gently and effectively. Fools argue. In contrast, in Jesus, we see a perfect example of how wise people can approach conversation.

In all three Proverbs we considered, we get a tiny glimpse of all the wisdom packed away in that collection of wise sayings. Ah, the glory of learning things the easy way by simply reading and adopting the wisdom of the ages. If you've never done so, I hope you will check out the book of Proverbs for yourself. You won't be disappointed.

As illustrated in these three Proverbs, and by our first US president, there's an etiquette to truth-telling. God's wisdom to us comes gently if we are willing to take responsibility in our reality, as we see with the woman at the well. While gentle with sinners, however, there were times when Jesus spoke sternly to those who suffered from religious hypocrisy. To practice the proper etiquette when we speak truth, we need to adopt humility and compassion in our hearts first, then let them flow off our tongues with our words, as well.

REWARD TRUTHFULNESS WITH COMPASSION

The woman at the well told the truth when Jesus asked her to go get her husband. Some commentators claim she was hedging by not blurting out her full history, but I know few women who would immediately share their most intimate details with a stranger, even a kind one. For this reason, I applaud her appropriate boundaries, not that anyone in Samaria in Jesus's day ever read a book on boundaries.

It seems so strange to demand more truth from others when they courageously share any part of a story, especially the excruciatingly painful parts. We can easily miss the fact that

Jesus chose to free her completely, not partially. Jesus had her best interests in heart. We often hesitate to hear every factual detail when we need to give freedom to those we love. We shy away from sharing the pain others feel. In doing so, we miss the freedom God intends to also give us.

THE PROBLEM WITH TRUTH

The problem with truth-seeking and truth-telling is that truth has a way of finding us. Just as a minor example, when I got to the earlier confession about my struggle to free myself of being argumentative and opinionated, I couldn't believe how hard it was to write it. My goodness! Who am I fooling? Everyone who knows me (or reads one of my books) can easily pick up on these tendencies. What folly to pretend it's not a chronic struggle for perfect ol' me. Ah, but the temptation is real.

On one hand, I know from experience when God's Spirit whispers to us about our sin, his voice is like water washing over us gently. On the other hand, when friends or family members tell us the truth, it tends to knock us down, like someone blasted us with a fire hose.

Those moments may even feel like a distorted misjudgment. When we adopt authenticity with humility, however, truth with compassion will inevitably begin to permeate all our relationships. Therefore, it's worth listening with an open heart to accept correction when it applies.

When she owned her truth about not having a husband, Jesus pressed in. He detailed her experience, "for you have had five husbands, and the one whom you now have is not your husband." Contrary to what we might expect, by making a complete truthful assessment, Jesus freed her completely.

TRUTH TAKES THE STING OUT OF THE PAST

How did Jesus free her with the truth? We know truth and freedom are deeply connected. For instance, John 8:32 tells us, "You shall know the truth and the truth shall make you free." For a heartrending example, the secret of abortion can freeze people in pain. Conversely, telling the story often frees those suffering and connects them to others who understand.

Fortunately, here in East Texas we have an amazing group called *Christ-centered Abortion Recovery and Education* (CARE).[4] *When* a person enters into one of the Bible studies facilitated by CARE, trauma begins to ebb away, and lives are reclaimed.

In confidential CARE studies, an interesting trend has emerged. Men and women often share they believe their churches will kick them out if they tell the truth about their abortions. Fortunately, the opposite is much more likely. We continually see churches embrace and comfort those affected by abortion.

Comforted hearts prove the redemptive power in relationships anchored in Jesus. Through CARE, fellow believers affirm Jesus's unconditional love and forgiveness. Fellowship with others springs up as we share. We gain freedom in truthful assessment. The loving comfort of others helps us heal.

"Healing happens in community, not isolation. Isolation is a place where the devil takes you so he can move in for the kill," counselor and minister Sandy Bristow pointed out on an *episode of Fireside Talk Radio*.[5]

Jesus verified his love for the woman at the well as he recounted the details of her experience. The woman found companionship with one who did not require her to hide. In fact, he stated the truth, respected the pain it represented, yet kept the conversation moving to his desired end. His goal was to confirm her authentically in his love with deepest compassion. He released her for the influence he prepared her to enjoy.

AUTHENTIC AND TRUTHFUL ABIDING LOVE

The sacred moment we witness in this passage of Scripture is holy companionship created by the Savior's willingness to love unconditionally and a woman's willingness to be authentic and truthful. In the most beautiful way, Jesus demonstrates his abiding love for the woman at the well. We witness her gracious release from the truth and pain surrounding her past. Oh, but this conversation could have been so different. How many times have we heard remarks that cut our hearts in two? Perhaps we've even been guilty of saying things that spoke volumes of rejection.

The human heart trembles in fear of rejection. What is rejection at its core? Condemnation. Condemnation says we are not good enough. *You are unworthy.* It may say some other version, like, *you failed, and, therefore, you are unworthy of companionship.* Nothing could be further from the truth, however, as Jesus brilliantly exposed. He profoundly touched her heart with the truth.

WHAT JESUS DID **NOT** DO

What Jesus *did not do* is important too. 1. He did not make excuses. 2. He did not blame others. 3. He did not list mitigating circumstances. 4. He did not minimize the painful truth of her situation.

No excuses. How often do we make excuses for our friends, rather than simply accepting their frailties? "Oh, you were just tired that day" or "You only spoke up because you were trying to help." In fact, we patronize our friends, offering a fake kind of grace and comfort, when we treat them like they need an excuse for failure. Is failure unacceptable without a good excuse? Of course not.

Truly loving each other means being adult-like about our shortcomings and loving each other anyway. My husband spends time in his studio making beautiful pottery. The imperfections in each piece are the secret of its value—each one is unmistakably a unique work of art. It is so with humans. Each of us is a unique work of art. Our frailties make us more beautiful to our Creator. In fact, we love gracefully when we love each other *because* of our imperfections.

No blame. It's also tempting to blame others as a way of comfort. "I only lost my temper because he said those mean things." In fact, blaming someone else when we lose our temper will not clear our conscience. To be free of the lingering guilt or shame of losing my temper, I must confess the truth, first to myself, then to God, then to the other person. Confession is a fancy church word for telling the truth, in order to take responsibility for our attitudes and actions.

No mitigating circumstances. Jesus did not list mitigating circumstances as we often do. "If only I had more money that month, I wouldn't have stolen the item" or "When I get that promotion, I'll treat my boss with more respect." Life is full of circumstances. We all mess up sometimes. Other people's choices adversely affect us. Jesus simply focused on the truth, without the dramatic details.

No minimizing. Finally, Jesus did not try to diminish the painful truth. Our true stories often include pain. Like Jesus, we too, can create moments of freedom, when we release others (or ourselves) by simply acknowledging the painful truth.

Have you been hurt in ways difficult to explain to anyone else? Is there something in your past with a painful grip on your emotions? Do you wish you could do it over again? I have wonderful news. Jesus loves you and me as he loved the woman at the well—unconditionally. This is not a superficial commitment, but one that goes core deep and includes every painful truth in your life.

Truth-filled love holds the promise of unconditional acceptance and value. Who could resist such an offer?

TRUTH WITHOUT REJECTION

Writing a book is a little like letting your best friends critique your children. It may be helpful, but it can hurt too. Plus, whether it's parenting or writing, too much criticism makes us all wonder if we have what it takes.

"I hope I'm not being too critical," wrote one friend, after taking precious time out of her schedule to read my manuscript and offer changes. She is the perfect example of trying to help with truth, while empathizing with the pain of the other person.

I may feel like a failure as editors sift through each and every word, but the truth is so different. In reality, every correction makes a better book for you, my reading friend. My heart welcomes their help.

Best of all, because they understand the struggle to produce the perfect word, perfect sentence, perfect book, editors offer their correction free of rejection or condemnation. Each truthful correction, without rejection, is a step toward the goal of creating a book worthy of you. Like writing a book, all meaningful conversational adventures boil down to mutual truth-sharing.

The woman responded with truth, and Jesus affirmed her decision. We can assume he did so without rejection, because she didn't end the conversation. Instead, she marveled at his astuteness. He rewarded her by pressing more deeply into her pain with tremendous compassion. Then, in a miraculous show of his mercy and goodness, he took the sting out of her past by accepting her, including all the details he knew about her past experiences.

Now she is ready to honor him with an accurate assessment of her own: here is a man like no other. A prophet? Wait until we look at the way he honors her with some amazing ideas about true spirituality and religious hypocrisy which we will explore in the next chapter.

Yet, as we will see, even in honoring him, she also circled back to her original objections. Did he ignore them again? I can't wait to look together at his surprising response.

BEST QUESTION ABOUT FACTUAL ASSESSMENTS

When we assess a situation factually to go on a truth-telling mission, what should we avoid?

We should avoid self-righteousness and condemnation. It's one thing to be Jesus and give someone a factual assessment, it's another thing to be a fellow sinner. We ruin the opportunity for meaningful conversation when we slam the other person with hard truth.

Beginning with a thoughtful question or story, for instance, can set a tone to engage the other person's imagination. The more factual we are, the more we improve the odds our conversational adventure will be a huge success. We can have a clear conscience if we do no further damage to the relationship. We can choose compassion and kindness even if it seems we failed to break through defenses.

The New Testament writers left out many details when they recorded Jesus's factual assessment of the woman's past. The disciples weren't witnesses to this part of the story, which begs a question. Who told them the details?

I suspect it was the woman herself, based on what she told the rest of her community. Was this her first-person account? By whatever means the story came to us, we can safely assume Jesus spoke to her with a world of compassion. Based on Jesus's example, compassion qualifies us to be people of influence as well as readiness. Condemnation disqualifies us.

PRACTICAL TIP: LIST THE RELEVANT FACTS

Tonight, list the facts, just the facts. After listing every relevant fact you can think of pertaining to the situation you wish to discuss, cut the list in half. Now, go back and cut it again. When you pare down to only two or three essential facts, stop. Stick to these essential facts as the basis for your conversational adventure.

God is all-knowing. Humans? Not so much. Conversations can quickly turn into arguments. Truth can be tricky, especially when two people are intensely committed to different perspectives. Mix in a little condemnation, and what an explosion.

If you feel in anyway impatient when making factual assessments, pause. Ask God to give you stamina so you can stick to the facts. Your success hinges on focus, patience, and tenderness.

MAY WE PRAY TOGETHER?

Dear Father in heaven, you call us into conversation with you through prayer. In the quiet moments we spend with you, we draw deeply on the spiritual insight and tenderness you offer. Such compassion is unavailable anywhere else. Thank you for loving us in our weakest, most selfish moments. Give us grace and dignity to handle the facts clearly and gently. Help us remember who we are: fellow travelers who face temptation daily. Keep us humble and tender, O Lord. Now, consider your child who wants to be effective in a difficult conversational adventure with a person who may not be able to hear. Bless this person because that's your heart's desire. In Jesus's name. Amen.

I have a theory about the human mind. A brain is a lot like a computer. It will only take so many facts, and then it will go on overload and blow up.—Erma Bombeck

CHAPTER 8:
CHANGE OF STATUS

How do we worship God, especially in authentic conversations?
By affirming the significance of others.

> The woman said to him, "Sir, I perceive that You are
> a prophet. Our fathers worshiped on this mountain,
> and you Jews say that in Jerusalem is the place
> where one ought to worship." Jesus said to her,
> "Woman, believe Me, the hour is coming when you
> will neither on this mountain, nor in Jerusalem,
> worship the Father. You worship what you do not
> know; we know what we worship, for salvation is of
> the Jews. But the hour is coming, and now is, when
> the true worshipers will worship the Father in spirit
> and truth; for the Father is seeking such to worship
> Him." (John 4:19–23)

A beautiful bride, all smiles, her handsome groom holds
her hand and grins back from the computer screen. Clicking
through the pictures, we see the joyful couple surrounded by
a whole community of loved ones. These two young people
begin their marital adventure saturated with support and
encouragement.

Then, on another page, we notice a recent new status:
single. The single status tells us worlds of hurt conspired to
break up a once happy couple.

Change of status conveys more than ever before in the era of social media. But why does status matter and where is true significance? Significance is a misrepresented, underrated commodity in today's world. Does status simply mean fame and fortune combined to create significance? The world would tell us so.

Even though status has very little to do with significance, we are infatuated with status. Sometimes, when I check my latest social media numbers for my work, I have flashbacks to junior high school. Oh, the strain of trying to be one of the cool kids.

We seem to live in a culture dedicated to status seeking. I don't know if social media invites more envy, more comparisons, and more feelings of being short-changed, but, certainly, status seeking is the opposite of resting in our own sense of significance.

Is a perfect past necessary for significance and influence? Thankfully, Jesus taught the opposite. He sat next to a woman and had a conversation. In doing so, he confirmed her significance despite whatever her past held.

The woman at the well rewarded Jesus's patience by recognizing his status step by step. First, she extended a title to him: prophet. While respectful, the title prophet was not what Jesus sought. Instead, he sought a relationship with her. He moved the conversation toward his goal by

- addressing her objections with clarity and respect,
- motivating her with a clear definition of true worship for all the ages, and
- inviting her to receive salvation and to change her status to true worshiper.

JESUS TREATED HER WITH RESPECT

Jesus saw a woman who had value designed into her very being. She was significant then as we are today. He loved this woman and desired companionship with her. He detoured from the Pharisees and "had to go to Samaria." Could it be he went for this one conversation with this one lady? He sought her out right where she was, getting water, going about her normal routine. Just another day in the life of a woman.

We can learn a lot by how Jesus exposed her readiness. We're not Jesus, so these lessons are crucial for us. For starters, we must make positive assumptions about the people God allows to cross our paths. God believes each person is significant and so should we. Granting status to other people reflects God's view of each person's value.

As they talked, she returned to objections about religious, political, and social customs. Especially in this passage, Jesus may seem to have flip-flopped. But what we see is a glorious communicator at work. While he ignored her first objections, now he answers her with clarity. We notice two things. 1. He waited until she was ready to receive the life-changing information he offered. 2. On the topic of worship, he provides her with serious information while treating her with respect.

SHE GRANTS JESUS PROPHET STATUS

Recognizing him as a prophet, she grants him a wee bit more status. He is no longer a stranger at her well, but a respected truth-teller, a prophet.

It's a courageous choice. By giving a title of authority, she is moving closer to a real relationship with him. Already she moved toward true worship, because she is beginning to understand who Jesus really is. It makes sense her next question has to do with worshiping God. Jesus, the Savior, is at her well. He's the only one who can fully meet her core needs.

What exactly did she need? On the surface, her need is for a stable family where she feels cherished. Even though we're unsure of her exact situation, her core need for respect, affection, and companionship seems to have gone unmet. Jesus saw her desire for a place of honor in stable companionship.

Jesus offered a kind of relationship stability the woman had not experienced. We stabilize all our relationships by granting status to others. To grant status to others means to respect the significance God sees in them, not worldly, temporary status. We may need to put aside our preconceived ideas if we want to appreciate the significance God gives each individual.

For instance, as modern Christians, we may be so calloused as to assume any person with good character is able to choose a stable home life. Sadly, that simply is not true. I love the way Pastor Bobby Dagnel of Lubbock First Baptist Church counseled me when I asked for his advice about this passage.

> To paint a lurid picture of this woman's life situation is an abuse of the text. At every reading of this narrative, I have considered the woman a victim—a victim of the social structure into which she was birthed; a victim of her own absence of self-worth; a victim of heartless men who divorced her or, as you have alluded, the victim of men's tragic deaths. In the absence of details, I would only wish that we would extend to her the same courtesy and genteel handling as did Jesus.[1]

I'm so grateful for this kind of compassionate and tempered wisdom among the countless good leaders I know, like Pastor Dagnel. There is only one righteous judge, Jesus. We must be very careful not to judge the woman at the well or anyone we meet. Instead, we can grant them significance based on God's unconditional love for each of us.

More than any time in history, we have opportunity to let go of any residual victim status mindset and choose something better. This woman set such a powerful example for all of us, no matter her past circumstances or traumas. She boldly laid claim to a better future. You gotta love her guts.

HANDLING OBJECTIONS WITH CLARITY

Next, she asserts her intelligence and restates a tough objection. Please note, she's not shy here when she honors Jesus as a truth-teller. Her observation holds him account- able for religious hypocrisy. "Our fathers worshiped on this mountain, and you Jews say that in Jerusalem is the place where one ought to worship" (John 4:20).

Her comment clarifies a distinction between the man-made religious solutions of her people and those who endorsed strict rules about worship in Jerusalem. Sniffing at the hypocrisy associated with man-made religiosity, she wants to know just exactly what kind of worship God finds acceptable. She certainly asked the right person about true worship.

Hypocrisy and religiosity are serious concerns for us all, even in modern times. Religiosity happens when we make up "spiritual" checklists to make us feel better about ourselves. Hypocrisy happens when we pretend to be more spiritual than we really are.

Her boldness inspires me to be less timid about what I ask Jesus. (Yes, after all these centuries, she is still influencing people. Wow!) She gets right to the point with Jesus, clearly stating her frustration. Since he is a spiritual teacher with a following, she holds him accountable. She was a bold, confident, and smart gal.

We know how frustrated Jesus got with hypocrisy, calling the Pharisees a brood of vipers. We can easily imagine his heart lit up with delight when she asked about true worship.

HE REDEFINES WORSHIP

He handled her question with a confident, firsthand knowledge of the problem. He even went so far as to redefine the concept of worship, putting aside the cultural definition altogether. (Calling her *woman* may sound disrespectful to modern ears, but here it's actually a term of respect, like Texans say *ma'am*.)

> Woman, believe Me, the hour is coming when you will neither on this mountain, nor in Jerusalem, worship the Father. You worship what you do not know; we know what we worship, for salvation is of the Jews. But the hour is coming, and now is, when the true worshipers will worship the Father in spirit and truth; for the Father is seeking such to worship Him. (John 4:21–23)

Jesus clarified God is not worshiped in man-made rituals and rules-keeping. Both traditions will be eliminated by virtue of Jesus's own death and resurrection. In fact, the destruction of the temple in Jerusalem is only a few years away as they talk.

We may ask the question, what does worshiping in spirit and truth mean? It means to put aside all pretensions of man-made perfection. By saying, "salvation is from the Jews," Jesus acknowledges centuries of prophetic truth predicting a coming Savior. He clarifies that worship means seeking the Savior who is already seeking each one of us.

We must run to a Savior who can set us free from sin. We can rest in deep companionship with him. Then, emboldened by his unfailing love for us, we can seek to love others unconditionally. To know God and to cherish a relationship with him is the beginning of worship. To love others in his honor is to worship him in our daily activities. Combining love for God and love for others is how we worship God in spirit and truth.

GRANTING HER SIGNIFICANCE DESPITE HER STATUS

There is a true way to worship God, which has nothing to do with a place and everything to do with our hearts. Perhaps she wondered why this stranger seemed so relaxed and confident when people often feel threatened by a serious question. Jesus readily reciprocates with truth, motivating her to think outside the box.

"The woman is intelligent, and Jesus takes her more seriously than would have been common in the first century. Not only is she intelligent, she is theologically astute. That's one of the things I really enjoy about this passage. It is a theological exchange, and Jesus invites her in, to the surprise of many," says Ben A. Simpson, Assistant Director of Spiritual Formation, George W. Truett Theological Seminary.[2]

Jesus did not condescend because she was a woman. Rather, he addressed her concerns with deep respect for her intelligence and her ability to process the information. He granted her significance despite her perceived low status because she was a woman and a Samaritan. He challenged her to think clearly and believe. He made the positive assumption she would be ready for the challenge. She did not disappoint. She responded with confidence in her ability to think through his insights.

She sought out solid teaching from him. Salvation is from the Jews, he tells her, implying it was available to all who were ready to receive it from them. Yep, even lowly Samaritans who come to the well alone. With beautiful sentiment, he clarifies that religion is one thing. Spirit and truth are radically something else altogether.

This rabbinical teacher discussed abstract religious doctrine with her as if she, too, were trained in rabbinical teaching. He treated her with respect as an intelligent person who could process the abstract information he disclosed. He assumed the very best, most positive outcome for her and, amazingly, she kept up with him. We marvel as we read her sacred story two thousand years later.

This is truly a respectful, positive way to engage people. We can grant people status, too, affirming their significance. Of course, we all know, sometimes people respond in ways that are hurtful and full of rejection. There is also an amazing place, however, where we trust others simply because we trust God. No longer dependent on other people's responses for our significance, we can step out in faith. Like Jesus, we can assume the other person will intelligently process any new information.

WORSHIP EXPRESSED IN SACRED STORIES

I witnessed a beautiful example of faith expressed in deeply authentic conversational adventure when I invited Doug McSwane on our show to talk about the suicide of his son.[3] Doug shared heartbreaking details of Patrick's battle with schizophrenia. I remember Patrick well as a darling little boy. As a loving young man, Patrick continued to bring his family much joy and delight, even as the disease took its toll.

Doug shares their story often, disregarding any possible negative consequences for him personally. For the McSwane family, speaking about the joy of Patrick's life and the loss they felt about his death, is an act of faith. Ignoring the risk of rejection, they've decided to absorb the deeply personal cost of making their tender, sacred story public.

The McSwanes are a perfect example of how making a positive assumption becomes a blessing. With courageous and positive hearts, the McSwanes assume other people will find much-needed help in their family's experience. This is not some kind of naïveté based on no reality. Instead, it is a deliberate decision to respect those who also suffer pain.

Doug makes the positive assumption someone in his audience will be ready for the truth he offers each time he speaks. He grants others the status of truth-seekers. As a result, many who hear their story are comforted and encouraged.

In telling of God's presence in their pain, the McSwanes truly worship God in their deepest spirit, honoring the beauty of his Spirit. A true story—with ramifications deeply affecting them in their most spiritual inner person—told to honor God. His Spirit stayed with them throughout the painful tragedy. God comforted them as they grieved and adjusted to life without their beloved son. Now they share their story as an act of faith and worship.

Making positive assumptions fuels our desire to worship God and to share his love with others. We know the God who seeks us out, loving us unconditionally, no matter our circumstances. So what if people reject us or the message we bring? We speak with tender boldness because we know the One whose unfailing love empowers us to love others. We know God.

In this account of their conversation, the woman at the well made a decision to know Jesus better. She took her confusion and frustration to him. She rejected religiosity and faux spirituality. Instead, she entered an intimate conversation with Jesus. He responded to her question about worship by talking about salvation. Would she change her status from alone to true worshipper? It would take a leap of faith. To prompt a response, Jesus points out God seeks true worshippers.

SEEKING TRUE WORSHIPPERS

Can we imagine the God of the universe who is seeking us out? If not for Jesus, this concept would surely be beyond our imagination. This is the unique truth that sets Christianity apart from all other religions. Other religions teach man's need to seek God. Christianity teaches God seeks us out through the life of his Son, Jesus Christ, just as Jesus himself sought out the woman at the well.

As Jesus touched lives all around him, his interactions always showed his own unity with God, his Father. God's Spirit poured out of Jesus's life, like life-giving water. The conversational adventure with the woman at the well is only one of countless examples. Many of his adventures were later recorded by his followers after his resurrection.

His disciples devoted themselves to creating a record of his life, inviting us to join them in relationship with Jesus. The Christ followers, who immediately took his message and his work of loving others upon themselves, became known as Christians. Their movement became a community, known as the Church, even as they lived in a variety of locations.

Through them, we receive this beautiful account and many other sacred stories of Jesus, written to include future generations of followers, like us. In this, we have community with those who went before us. Jesus still seeks us out through them and their writing. We, in turn, extend his offer of companionship to others.

Jesus said, "The Father is seeking." (John 4:23). *Seeking* is a significant word in the passage. The woman who came to the well alone began to realize her dream of meeting the Savior is within reach. He came to her well, seeking her.

As tempting as it may be to judge Christianity by us Christians, Jesus's arrival as a human sets Christianity apart. Jesus's loving sacrifice on the cross and history-changing resurrection still restores and changes lives today. Christianity teaches God seeks us and provides for our spirituality himself. Other religions teach people to seek God by working hard to please him, through a list of religious checkpoints. In contrast, Christianity teaches we respond in joyful gratitude to the God who seeks *us* out.

"Even as Christians, we think if we talk about a place of weakness, it means we have a lack of faith. When really the fact that we all need Christ desperately is the whole premise of being a Christian," Dana Goodrum, author of *Open with Your Broken*, said when I interviewed her. "There's purpose in the pain, purpose in the struggles, beauty in everybody's broken."[1] We all have sacred stories, sometimes painful ones, but they are not the end of our story.

THE WELL

I firmly believe God's ultimate purpose for each one of us enfolds two truths: God wants to have eternal companionship with each of us, and he wants to help us remake our lives to reflect his glory so others will join us in the journey of companionship. To worship him in spirit and truth means we must draw deeply into our own spirits—trusting his Spirit—for the authentic conversations we crave. Oh, what beautiful influence to call others into companionship with God.

We may believe we're insignificant because past mistakes have disqualified us in some way. Instead, we must make positive assumptions about all people, even ourselves. As we do, we demonstrate faith. God believes each person is significant. Do we believe it? Do you believe you are significant? I hope so because it is true.

Just like the woman at the well, each one of us is inherently significant because God seeks a relationship with each of us, thus proving our value. I like to equate our value to the way my grandmother shopped a sale at a huge department store in Fort Worth, Texas.

WHO DOESN'T LOVE A SALE?

The shiny, modern tram took us to the big city department store from the pasture-like parking lot a few blocks away, a thrilling adventure for a little kid. If you grew up in New York City, you have no idea how exciting a subway-like ride through a tunnel to a glamorous store could be for a country girl.

Once at our destination, we proceeded past the full-priced clothing directly to the basement. All the great bargains were piled unto tables with raised edges. Store-bought clothes thrilled me. I was too young to appreciate the designer nature of my hand-crafted wardrobe.

My grandmother was never content to pay the marked-down price. Oh, no. Instead, she always checked with the cashier to see if it couldn't be "knocked off just a wee bit more" due to some perceived flaw. Meme was a fabulous seamstress and could fix anything.

What does Meme's shopping technique have to do with human value? Simply this—in all those years of shopping in the basement, I never once heard my grandmother say, "Even though this garment is flawed and stained, I insist on paying full price for it." Yet, in our most utterly worthless condition, in our darkest moment, when we have even rejected ourselves, God reaches down and chooses each one of us.

God sent his own beloved Son to pay full price for each one of us. His own life in exchange for ours. Unlike the picked-over garments left on a sale table, God sees our humanity—including our scars, wounds, frailties, and, yes, our human tendency to sin—as part and parcel of our value to him. His ability to rise from death demonstrates his ultimate power. He is so powerful he can repair whatever needs attention in our hearts, just as surely as my grandmother could remake any garment with her sewing mastery.

Meme loved to recreate a garment, taking trusted fabric and design to a whole new level of current style. In fact, sometimes my grandmother's recreations were superb improvements to the original version. God, likewise, loves to recreate us, often into someone even better than we could have ever imagined.

If God did not spare his own son, but gave his beloved life for us instead, how much more should we see the value in each other? With this understanding, we can choose to embrace one another's significance, even when it's a challenge to do so.

God seeks us out. This blows me away every time I think about it. Best of all, as we cherish him, he cherishes our worship. When we honor him by serving others, he is happy. I know, I know. I sound like a kid saying it that way, but I like the thought of my heart making God's heart happy. I bet you do, too.

BEST QUESTION ABOUT SIGNIFICANCE

What happens when we grant status to others, honoring their significance?

Granting true status—significance—to others stabilizes all our relationships. We grow in understanding of our own significance as we respect the value of others. Best of all, when we cultivate the habit of assuming the best about other people, granting ourselves grace gets easier too.

"For with what judgment you judge, you will be judged; and with the measure you use, it will be measured back to you" (Matthew 7:2). Here's an important truth: We bind ourselves to self-condemnation when we judge and condemn others. By the way, if we know folks who habitually judge and condemn, it's okay to grant them some compassion since they probably suffer from self-condemnation.

With grace, we can habitually assume the truth: God loves the person with whom we are trying to communicate. This, then, is faith in action—to know God and bring others into community with him is true worship.

Worship is responding to the price tag God put on us—the life, death, and resurrection of his beloved Son—by serving others with compassion and joy.

Practical Tip: Your Personal Self-Talk

Today, consider your own personal self-talk. Do you feel handicapped by your story, your past, or any other perceived limits? If so, begin releasing yourself from residual self-condemnation. Make a list of friends who offer you respect, affection, and companionship. In these gifts, they grant you status and affirm your significance. Pray about whether it's time to share any painful stories with a trustworthy, judicious friend.

Oh, how we suffer with negative self-talk. We often forget to encourage our own hearts as we encourage others. Our imagination conjures the sick, slow poison of negative thoughts. Please, practice self-compassion. Why not make some positive assumptions about yourself today? Grant yourself some status. In this way, you'll agree with God who already loves you exactly as you are.

Ironically, the more aware I became of my negative assumptions and self-talk, the more I condemned myself for being negative. It's funny to me now, but it wasn't fun at the time. Granting forgiveness and grace is hard work, especially to ourselves. Yet, this is a worshipful way to serve others. It's also a healthy way to treat ourselves.

Drawing deeply means understanding how valuable our own humanity is to God. Faith is born when we trust we are significant to God—enough to send his Son to seek us. Why condemn yourself or anyone else for not being a perfect little demigod? Being perfectly human means being imperfect. God's divinity is magnified in our humanity. His righteousness in the gift of salvation.

MAY WE PRAY TOGETHER?

Dear Father in heaven, you created us to have a relationship with you. We want to know you in a real and significant way. You have already proven our worthiness by seeking us out to love. Help us to assume the best about others and ourselves. Forgive us our sins, particularly of self-rejection, and help us as we forgive others. Empower us to trust the significance you offer us. Give us grace to have pure hearts in order to make wise choices.

Thank you, O Lord, for making salvation available to us when we accept your gift. You see us, you hear us always, and we are grateful. Like the woman at the well, you share tender truth with us to pass along. You respect our intellect and our ability to understand what you offer. If this person does not know you as Savior, together we ask for you to reveal the truth of your saving, sacrificial love. Help us to be true worshipers. Bless us now because that's your heart's desire. In Jesus's name. Amen.

"We love Him because He first loved us." —1 John 4:19

CHAPTER 9:

BRING A BUCKET OF TRUTH

HOW CAN WE BRING A BUCKET OF TRUTH?
BY OWNING GOD'S DESIGN FOR US AS VESSELS OF TRUTH.

> "God is Spirit, and those who worship Him must
> worship in spirit and truth." The woman said to
> Him, "I know that Messiah is coming (who is called
> Christ). When He comes, He will tell us all things."
> (John 4:24–25)

Giggling, two of my friends ran up from behind to catch a lovely blonde, assuming it was Taylor Swift. We were in Nashville. You just never know what might happen. We were ready with questions and a camera, until the blonde turned around and— you guessed it—not Taylor. (Taylor, if you're reading this, I have some friends with questions about literacy for you.)

Even though the woman at the well never heard of Taylor Swift, she dreamed of meeting a special person. She watched for the Messiah, a Savior, whom she was convinced would come. What a woman! Don't you want to be friends with this gal?

Some might be skeptical. Not this woman. She was totally prepared to meet the one and only Savior of the universe, whenever he happened to drop by. She was ready, and Jesus did not disappoint. He transformed her from alone to influential and plugged into her community. How did he do it? Can we do it too?

Yes. God intends for us to be influential in our own unique way. Plus, women have a specific design attribute we often overlook. Yet, this quality is truly valuable in any community. We inherited this beautiful attribute long ago from our fore mother Eve. In this chapter, we will look at how women are specifically designed by God to love truth and seek wisdom.

If you are a woman, you'll love this. If you are a man—especially if you love a wife, a daughter, a sister, or a mother—this information is essential and perhaps thrilling. If you are the parent of a daughter, you may be especially comforted, particularly if you teach her to value her design for the sake of her own well-being. Pastors and leaders may rethink their commitment to include women in any and all conversations.

Let's check out how the woman at the well embraced her own design as a vessel of truth. We'll see how Jesus taught the woman to get a whole lot more out of life by

- clarifying the significance of God's Spirit,
- understanding her natural desire for wisdom,
- exposing the fragile nature of truth,
- recognizing her design as a vessel of pure truth, and
- appealing to her deepest heart's desire for companionship.

JESUS CLARIFIED THE SIGNIFICANCE OF GOD'S SPIRIT

In the last chapter, we examined how respecting the significance of each person stabilizes relationships. Sometimes, though, we have trouble grasping how significant God's Spirit is in our relationship with him. Now, we'll see why women have an uncanny knack for getting to the point when it comes to truth.

Since spirit and truth are connected and emphasized by Jesus, knowing what the words mean is important. Truth is the nonnegotiable, factual reality. In our post-modern way of thinking, it can be hard to believe anything is absolute truth. Yet, we know many abstract concepts are true even though the actuality has little physical form, like love or peace. In our deepest heart, we know love and peace exist. Plus, we see evidence of love and peace in a baby's smile, for example. Love and peace are truths we experience deep within our spirits.

In another example, the sound of wind and the movement of the trees let us know when the wind blows. We cannot see the wind, but we know it truly exists. Jesus compared God's Spirit to the wind when he privately explained two births to Nicodemus, a Pharisee (John 3:1–17). In the first birth, we are born as babies into the physical world. God's Spirit ushers those who choose him into a second birth of eternal, heavenly reality, according to Jesus.

"The wind blows where it wishes, and you hear the sound of it, but cannot tell where it comes from and where it goes. So is everyone who is born of the Spirit" (John 3:8).

To know God and enter an authentic conversation with him, we must understand he is Spirit. He invites us to enter into a second birth when we allow his Spirit to join ours, abiding together in our innermost heart, or spirit.

One of God's most notable qualities or identities is his Spirit. To know God and worship him we must cherish the beauty of his Spirit. Many books have been written about God's Spirit, and I encourage you to read them voraciously.

I like what Merrill F. Unger writes about how God's Spirit "moves upon the hearts and consciences of all men, attending revealed truth with His power wherever it is known and even where it is not known, affording some measure of divine light and gracious influence (Acts 2:17; John 16:7–11; I Cor. 2:4)."[1] God's Spirit moving upon our hearts must surely be one of the most profound, authentic conversations we can ever experience.

Spiritual Companionship

The idea of spirit can seem so abstract we might think it's beyond human perception. Surprisingly, the concept of spiritual identity is easy for us to grasp. Perhaps because our hearts whisper the truth: *We are spiritual creatures designed for spiritual companionship.*

Have you ever had a rousing conversational adventure with an atheist or agnostic? These are some of my favorite people on earth, mainly because they are so honest about the way their views differ from mine. What a beautiful place to start a conversation—with no pretense.

In those stimulating conversations, I always try to ask one of my favorite questions, "Do you believe you have a spirit?" Without exception, people always answer yes. We all understand the abstract concept of our inner person. Even those who question the existence of God embrace the idea of our own imperishable essence—called our spirit.

In our innermost recesses, we all crave emotionally intimate relationships when we can share ourselves openly at our deepest level without fear of rejection. What we really crave is a spiritual connection, like the one Jesus offered the woman at the well. For instance, we rejoice when friends patiently love us without condition, especially when they know the truth about our frailties.

Healthy families and true friends give us all the time and opportunity we need to grow in understanding and wisdom. They accept us when we make mistakes, as all humans are prone to do. They may even hold us accountable to reach our potential. We know we are cherished.

Our spirit is the place where unfailing love and deep truth register. That's why Jesus's conversation with the woman at the well feels authentic to us. He draws deeply to speak to the woman about things that resonate in her inner self. He is inviting her into spiritual companionship with him by way of this deep conversation. I am convinced our spirits are designed to be a reflection of his Spirit. We are made in his image, especially because we have a spirit.

To worship God in spirit and truth is a way of cherishing him, honoring his truthful Spirit in our hearts. We become his companion in this life and the next. We put aside hypocrisy and present our unvarnished hearts at the mercy of his acceptance or rejection. In this way, the word *Savior* becomes a blessed relief, especially for those of us who tremble at the thought of such vulnerability.

WISDOM NATURALLY APPEALS TO WOMEN

Perhaps, the woman at the well viewed herself as a woman alone, a second-class Samaritan. Nevertheless, she had some opinions about the coming Savior. She was interested in learning more about him and the promises associated with his coming. In fact, I suspect she had prepared herself so she would recognize him. You know, she was ready just in case she accidentally met up with him in some unlikely place. Like, say, the well. In fact, she doesn't say *if* he comes. She says, "*When* He comes, He will tell us all things" (John 4: 25, italics mine). *When*, not *if*.

Plus, she says he'll tell all things. *All* things. Wow! That's a big perception. Clearly, she's given his coming some serious imaginative thought. This is a woman who seeks knowledge, even wisdom.

With her desire to meet a Savior who could tell us all things, my mind jumps back to the Garden of Eden when the serpent tempted Eve with these words: "For God knows that in the day you eat of it your eyes will be opened, and you will be like God, knowing good and evil" (Genesis 3:5). Another big perception. In this case, the woman Eve accepted the temptation, revealing how motivated she was to have knowledge—especially the difference between good and evil.

Women are designed by God to be seekers and communicators of truth. It's in our DNA. It's a chromosomal double X kind of thing. This is important information whether you're female or male. Women ought to be free to own our influence. For men, as leaders in homes, especially if you have a mother, sisters, a wife, or daughters, you'll want to pay close attention to the way Satan tempted Eve and why.

God designed women specifically to be people who love wisdom. You better believe our enemy the devil knows this to be true, even if we fail to recognize this truth. Women are vessels of truth under attack by an enemy who wants to minimize our potential for pure influence because the devil hates our designer.

Wise people won't balk at hearing truth spoken, particularly by strong females. I like the way Cynthia Ulrich Tobias describes the advantage of SWW (Strong-Willed Women) against the enemy in her book, *A Woman of Strength and Purpose*.

The Enemy would have us think that it's wrong to possess strong will. He tries to make us feel guilty for using it or to discourage us from speaking up, especially in the church. That's because he knows that when strong will is voluntarily given to God and used for His purposes, it becomes a mighty force for God. Can you imagine how quickly the Enemy has to flee when faced with groups of godly, strong-willed women coming together to pray? Do you think these women will be reluctant to step up and fight injustice, crime, or any other evil? Will they be afraid to stand against what's wrong or be daunted by seemingly impossible tasks? I don't think so. We won't all be called to fight in the same way—some will be on the front lines; others will prefer to work in the background—but every SWW serving God will play a critical role in carrying out His mission.[2]

Many of us are strong-willed but don't realize what a powerful force for good that can be. Under the guidance of God's own beautiful Spirit, there are no limits to the power he can unleash in us. If you combine a strong will, a compassionate heart, and an aptitude for truth, what do you get? A mighty force for good.

Have you ever noticed some people are magnets for the truth? It's like they can't help but say the one thing everyone else is too polite to mention. Or, worse, they notice when our attitude is bad. Have you ever felt like life has kicked you in the gut? These people seem to find us and get right to the point even when we are doing our best to hide away and lick our wounds alone. They ask all the intrusive questions. Lord, have mercy! They remind me of the treasure seekers of my childhood.

TRUTH DETECTORS

When I was a kid, we lived on Galveston Island in a little bungalow only a few blocks from the beach. Many happy days were spent chasing sandpipers and looking for shells. Of all the marvels on the beach, one thing stood out to me as a small child. Many treasure seekers skimmed the sand with metal detectors. *Beep! Beep! Beep!* Happy sounds and flying sand marked the spot as they dug for treasures. I imagined Jean Lafitte's hidden pirate's chest could be revealed with a metal detector at any moment.

I shared my excitement for the hunt with retired folks who carried buckets of loot. Their prime hunting time was each Monday morning after weekend tourists headed back to Houston and beyond. One day, an elderly gentleman astonished me by handing me the buried coin he'd found. Overwhelmed with gratitude and enthusiasm, I pestered Mom for a metal detector of my own. Alas, I lost interest before Christmas when childhood dreams, especially ones with loud beeps, had a slightly better chance of coming true.

Jesus promises if we seek truth, we will find it. "Ask, and it will be given to you; seek, and you will find; knock, and it will be opened to you. For everyone who asks receives, and he who seeks finds, and to him who knocks it will be opened" (Matthew 7:7–8). Of course, Jesus himself is the truth, so even in these words he is yet again offering a relationship with God to the many who listened that day. And to us.

Call me crazy, but I am every bit as wild about truth-seeking now as I was about metal detectors as a kid. Part of my child-like heart marvels that God would entrust something so rare and valuable into our hands simply because we looked for it.

In fact, the reason we created Camp Krafve was to spread as much truth as humanly possible with God's help. But we felt self-conscious about claiming to know truth, despite God's innumerable promises in Scripture to teach us truth and give us wisdom. Still, it felt like too big of an undertaking to actually claim to know truth. We wanted a cutline that expressed our optimism yet contained a little humility. That's how we came up with our "Truth with a Texas Twang" cutline. If you think we were motivated by pure insecurity—because Texans are not known for humility—you'd be right.

Of course, if you are a Christian, you probably treasure a strong desire to seek knowledge, truth, and wisdom too.

Sometimes folks go so far as to claim their opinions are truth. These days, opinion gets confused with truth, knowledge, and wisdom. But if we must choose only one, let's choose truth. Here's why.

SEEKING WISDOM: HARD-WIRED INTO A WOMAN'S HEART

Folks like to say knowledge is power. Knowledge is a good thing, right? However, knowledge can be misused to manipulate people. Truth is fragile. Simply stated, Jesus is the embodiment of truth, therefore we must be careful not to stray from his Spirit if we desire to be vessels of truth. When God's Spirit is disregarded, knowledge and fear are frequently used together to entrap people.

We can take a cue from Satan's provocative ability to pinpoint our vulnerabilities. This intrigues me: The devil got to Eve even before she had kids. Interesting, isn't it? Satan targeted her purpose before she understood it herself.

Eve was a unique creature in God's garden. Potentially fruitful and influential in ways scarcely imaginable. She is the mother of all who follow, including us. Therefore, the enemy zeroed in on her without mercy. She caved into the temptation about gaining special knowledge. Perhaps we can relate. For instance, my desire to help my husband in my own way can easily overpower my trust in God's care.

We know Eve shared this story—her sacred story—because it comes down to us from her perspective. When Eve retold this incident, she revealed a profound truth. Her primary interest wasn't in knowledge at all. She craved wisdom.

"So when the woman saw that the tree was good for food, that it was pleasant to the eyes, and a tree desirable to make one *wise*, she took of its fruit and ate" (Genesis 3:6, italics mine). However, what Satan offered was knowledge, not wisdom. "For God knows that in the day you eat of it your eyes will be opened, and you will be like God, *knowing* good and evil" (Genesis 3:5, italics mine).

What Eve really wanted was wisdom. Too bad she didn't think through the difference between knowledge and wisdom first. Yet, we can sympathize with her well-meaning instincts and can recognize the impatience that prompted her to act without judicious consideration.

Knowledge can be a good thing. Take, for instance, a surgeon's knowledge of the human body as he makes that first cut into his patient's flesh. We all want a doctor with tremendous knowledge.

For an example highlighting wisdom, consider a patient in hospice. A knowledgeable doctor will know all the physical signs of impending death, the loss of appetite, the veined knees, and the shallow breathing. However, a wise doctor will also understand with great compassion the enormous feeling of loss all those who love the patient experience. Wisdom will instruct such a doctor as he tenderly listens and ministers to the dying patient and the grieving family.

Knowledge only goes so far, wisdom goes further. To understand how fragile truth can be, we must know the difference between truth, knowledge, and wisdom.

The words knowledge and wisdom each have nuanced meanings. Knowledge is to acquire information based on observable data and patterns. Wisdom is to understand and live by the most important principles in life, then use understanding well in the interest of others. Because truth is nonnegotiable reality, the slightest distortion can create falsehood.

We've all experienced a moment when we heard someone make a factual statement, only to have the truth so distorted it became a falsehood. Kids are notorious for creating falsehoods out of truths. "Dad, Mom said we could go out for ice cream." Yes, but the child neglected to include the rest of the truth—after homework was done and chores finished.

If Eve had considered the difference between knowledge and wisdom, she might have better resisted the devil's scheme. Satan mixed just a wee distortion in with some factual information, and, lo and behold, a convincing lie was born. As a woman, I certainly relate to Eve's seemingly insatiable desire for wisdom.

Wisdom is a necessary species survival skill. Just ask any mother, and I bet she agrees. Raising human offspring requires wisdom. And lots of it. Knowing good and evil appealed to Eve. Ironically, as she sought wisdom, she simultaneously disregarded the truth in the warning God gave for her own safety and well-being.

She most likely received the directive through her husband, or perhaps from both Adam and God. In fact, God issued his warning directly to Adam before Eve was created. "And the Lord God commanded the man, saying, "Of every tree of the garden you may freely eat; but of the tree of the knowledge of good and evil you shall not eat, for in the day that you eat of it you shall surely die" (Genesis 2:16–17).

The Fragile Nature of Truth

Despite such dire consequences, Eve views wisdom as within reach and makes a quick, independent grab. Instead of wisdom, she's getting knowledge. Ouch! Here again, we see the fragile nature of truth. Often, other sensible people might slow us down before we make impulsive, ill-advised decisions. In this case, Adam joins in with Eve's folly after the fact.

Somehow, I am comforted to recognize I am not alone. I join Eve in my compulsion to satisfy my longing for wisdom with a poor substitute. Still, even in our most misguided moments, our hearts are designed to seek wisdom and share insight.

This compulsion we have as women to seek wisdom is addressed in 1 Peter 3:7 where husbands are counseled to give their wives honor "as the weaker vessel." We've all sat in pews as brave pastors tried to explain that verse without tripping over the ire of the women of the church, especially their own wives.

The fragile nature of truth is reflected in the fragile nature of its vessels. In Eve's case, knowledge seemed so desirable to her she was willing to go directly against God's instructions. In fact, she didn't pause long enough to care if the devil offered her knowledge, not wisdom.

The fragile nature of truth makes it susceptible to contamination. Truth can become deadly when it is polluted with even a tiny bit of falsehood, like a delicious cake with a tad bit of hemlock added. The crafty enemy of our souls appealed to Eve's natural desires, offering her something close to, but not quite, what her heart craved. With a drop of lie, he polluted the whole.

WHEN A WOMAN'S TRUTH DETECTOR GETS OUT OF WHACK

Like Eve, women are natural magnets for wisdom, sounding the alarm whenever truth is involved. Mishandle a woman, though, and her truth detector may get all out of whack. For instance, fathers who foster their daughters' trust will be comforted when their daughters' hearts are accurately gauged to truth.

When a woman is hurt or taken for granted, however, she can learn to distrust her own instincts. Perhaps this is why God commands men to cherish the wife as the weaker vessel. By cherishing their wives, husbands nurture trustworthy truth and wisdom in the hearts of their wives. The command to cherish your wife has a warning with it—so that the husband's "prayers may not be hindered" (1 Peter 3:7).

Bitterness or envy skew our truth detector, triggering inaccurate information. For example, when a wife's truth detector is out of whack, her husband may be at a greater disadvantage in knowing how he should pray, since she may hesitate to speak up with confidence. Like a broken metal detector, her inner beeper may fail to signal truth to her own heart. Her insecurity or pain may cause her to hesitate in giving her hubby valuable insight.

Unlike knowledge and wisdom, which are accessible to humans, truth is more elusive. Opinions interfere with our relationship with truth. Our best hope of understanding truth is in Jesus himself. Since truth is embodied in Jesus, there is a sacrificial element to truth. Plus, truth sets us free. When we meet people who have acquired wisdom, they often reflect a kind of sacrificial love and unhindered joy associated with truth, that is, with Jesus himself.

What's the difference between wisdom and knowledge then? Wisdom, like truth, must have that element of sacrificial understanding, whereas knowledge can simply be data collection. While we're on the topic of how knowledge and truth relate to each other, though, we don't want to forget that data collection can be an act of worship, too.

For instance, in the case of modern researchers who study post-traumatic stress disorder (PTSD), their knowledge and data gathering enable better treatments for those who suffer. Thus, researchers devote themselves to gathering data that serves others. So, even factual data, or knowledge, becomes wisdom when it's truthfully used to serve others sacrificially and compassionately.

We cannot self-centeredly seek wisdom. Everyone wants to be wise, I guess, but who wants to be unselfish? It seems wisdom and unselfishness go together. Anytime we selfishly seek wisdom—that is, independently from God—we risk damaging all our relationships, as we see in Eve's case.

THE WEAKER VESSEL: DESIGNED TO HOLD PURE TRUTH

Because the 1 Peter verse links effective prayer to honoring wives as the weaker vessel, maybe we could pause and ask a simple question. What does Peter mean by saying wives are the weaker vessel? I believe "weaker" here references the idea of women as vessels of truth.

Keeping in mind Eve's decision to pursue knowledge independent of God's guidance, perhaps a wife's weaker status has to do with our human tendency to move ahead impulsively without regard to God's instruction. In other words, we ignore his Spirit's whispering in our hearts. There are many times when we trust our fleshly tendencies to our own discredit.

I've lost count of all the times I've said something unthoughtful or unkind on an impulse. Especially when David and I were newly married, I caused my gentle-hearted, discreet husband no end of embarrassment. Even if my comment was true, I often messed up by saying things too bluntly. Now, when David kicks me gently under the table, I close my mouth instantly. He knows me so well. I always thank him later for rescuing me from my own indiscretions of the mouth.

As women are designed to be vessels of truth, our very nature hinges on understanding truth in the purest way humanly possible. Understanding pure truth would be impossible if not for God's own Spirit. Maybe the idea of a weaker vessel is not about judging the vessel, although I am the first to admit I often feel very weak. Instead, perhaps the concept emphasizes the fragile nature of truth itself, reflected in the fragile nature of a woman's heart.

We get a clue about how quickly truth can be transformed into a lie in the quick work the devil made of truth when he lied to Eve. One little distortion, and voila! A believable lie emerged, disguised as the truth. Eve believed the lie because it had the ring of truth about it.

As women, being a vessel of truth means it's imperative that we seek truth and handle it with purity and compassion, as Jesus did. Truth is a beautiful but fragile treasure and can be easily mishandled or distorted by selfish motives. At this point in my life, as an older woman, I wonder if the word "weaker" in 1 Peter 3:7 might be linked with our desire to seek knowledge independently of God and, perhaps, pridefully.

I also wonder if, in the modern church, women have been underestimated as creatures who are naturally wired to seek wisdom and truth. For example, wives can be discouraged from offering their husband insight by well-meaning friends who say, "wives should not be their husbands' Holy Spirit." Of course, God's Spirit, his living water, is available to fill all willing human vessels. God's Spirit is faithful to counsel our husband directly as wise wives often notice.

For that matter, our children, too, must be trained to directly access God's own dear Spirit for wisdom. Certainly, though, he also uses our carefully chosen insight to encourage those we love. While God does not need us to play Holy Spirit in each other's lives, he frequently uses us to gently and confidently share truth with each other. As daughters, sisters, friends, aunts, nieces, wives, and mothers, we are uniquely suited to tenderly implore those we love to seek and cherish truth too.

Life and family are not a competition between spouses. In families, men have their own specific, essential roles, talents, and gifts. As women, knowing God intends for us to love truth and seek it out offers us confidence. This natural tendency to desire wisdom and truth is a blessing to our husbands, friends, families, churches, communities ... everyone.

From the beginning, even before she had kids, Eve desired wisdom, "the woman saw that the tree was ... desirable to make one *wise*" (Genesis 3:6, italics mine). Seeking wisdom, a skill set wired into her DNA, would help her fulfill God's command to be fruitful and multiply.

We are Eve's daughters. We crave wisdom. Whether we are physical mothers who've given birth or emotional and spiritual mothers who've adopted those who need a mom, it matters not. Women enjoy a natural desire to understand truth, acquire wisdom, and pass it along. Thankfully, God deals individually with us, respecting our free will and making room for our choices, even the regrettable ones, as he did with Eve.

Fortunately, too, he blesses the man who has a wife. "He who finds a wife finds a good thing, And obtains favor from the Lord" (Proverbs 18:22). Husbands who cherish truth, often offered by their wives, are wise indeed. "Houses and riches are an inheritance from fathers, But a prudent wife is from the Lord" (Proverbs 19:14). Single, married, or widowed, our status as women includes God's design to make us seekers of wisdom, a lovely attribute women inherited from our first and foremost forebear, Eve.

The woman at the well is a perfect example of a truth seeker. In fact, she's seeking the greatest truth of all, the Savior. This woman, who came to the well alone, left with the greatest promise of fellowship and companionship ever offered to mankind. Man or woman, adult or child, we can rejoice in the hope this offers us all.

THINK ON THESE THINGS

As a truth seeker, the woman at the well meditated on the right stuff. She'd been pondering what it would be like if the Savior came to her village. Imagine the woman going about her daily activities, perhaps suffering rejection or sorrow. Yet, all the while, her mind is contemplating a Savior.

Like her, we can begin to harness our thoughts and retrain

them by contemplating what gives us hope and joy. To get our minds on straight, I like the advice Paul includes in his letter to the Christians at Philippi, who were severely persecuted:

> Finally, brethren, whatever things are true, whatever things are noble, whatever things are just, whatever things are pure, whatever things are lovely, whatever things are of good report, if there is any virtue and if there is anything praiseworthy—meditate on these things. The things which you learned and received and heard and saw in me, these do, and the God of peace will be with you. (Philippians 4:8–9)

True, noble, just, pure, lovely, good news, virtue, praise-worthy—that's quite a list!

Until I read that verse, it never occurred to me I had a choice about my thoughts. To be people of influence, especially in a culture that obsesses about status, we simply must get our minds into a place where we are focused on what is positive and true.

Truth seeking is serious business, starting with the truth about ourselves. We can't afford to waste our energy feeling defeated or unworthy. Nor can we afford to get swept up into the temptation to measure our own status against anyone else's—a form of envy. Jesus demonstrated this truth when he spoke to the woman alone at the well.

COMPANIONSHIP: OUR HEART'S DEEPEST DESIRE

The Savior sought her out in her lonely circumstances, her self-doubt, and her prejudiced understanding of her status. Jesus took a weary moment and turned it into a miracle. He expanded her understanding of spirit and truth because he understood her heart's deepest desire for companionship.

Therefore, when he offered her living water, miraculously, she claimed it. This same Savior cares for each one of us, no matter our circumstances or how we perceive ourselves. He offers to make us people of influence too. Like the woman at the well, we can bring buckets of refreshing truth to those we love.

Although she brought an empty bucket to the well, she eventually *became* the bucket. First, she came to fill her water pot with water from Jacob's well. Then, to her heart's complete satisfaction, to the blessing of her whole community, and to God's glory forever, she moved onto the next stage of influence. She filled the ready bucket of her heart, then she invited others to drink from the living water she discovered. Once she glimpsed true companionship with the Savior, she instantly shared the invitation.

Jesus offered to give her living water. She claimed it. She didn't hide her full heart away and think about when a good time would be to talk about this with her closest, most trusted friends. No sir-ee! With joy overflowing, her heart boldly splashed this beautiful truth out to everyone she knew, starting with her community's leaders. Thus, she worshiped God in spirit and truth.

To be prepared, we must have ready hearts. We must be watching with expectation for truth. We must recognize truth when we see it. Truth is a fragile treasure and we must handle it with humble gratitude. Ready hearts, humbly seeking truth, qualify us to be people of influence.

Best Question about Your Bucket

How do I fill my bucket?

We get weary, just as surely as the woman grew weary from all those trips to the well to refill her water pot. Jesus promised the woman at the well something so unimaginable she might as well have been trying to imagine a dishwasher or indoor plumbing. Living water does flow freely, but only to those prepared to receive it. Seeking truth means searching for it. There are simply no shortcuts.

Fortunately for us, we have the priceless gift of the Scriptures available for our personal devotion. Both Old and New Testaments constitute a massive collection of amazing, truthful treatises on all aspects of life. The eyewitness accounts of Jesus's life on earth are our best sources of truth. In those accounts, we discover more and more about the true nature of living water, that is, God's Spirit.

Additionally, we are not lone rangers. Living alongside us are men and women who have walked with God so long their lives refresh us and overflow with living water. Meanwhile, many scholars thrill to answer our most challenging questions, in person or via the internet. With so much truth available to us, how could we fail to ready our hearts?

Most importantly, God's own dear Spirit is available to guide us as we pursue our relationship with him (John 14:15–17).

Still, we can't help but notice our bucket sometimes feels just plain empty even as we know Jesus more and more. We turn to God to refill our emotional buckets, trusting his Spirit and his truth. Then, we'll be prepared to continually pour out wisdom on those we love.

We gain beloved companions to help us stay the course. Together we share this life in community and celebrate in eternity forever. We fill our hearts, like buckets, with the joy of companionship, with knowledge of his truth through the Scriptures, and with moments alone with Jesus. All the while, his Spirit and love splash around in our hearts until good stuff is bound to slosh out.

The more we study the idea of truth in Scripture, the more we understand that God designed women particularly to be vessels of truth. Here's one more beautiful truth. Women are not the only descendants of Eve. All people, men and women, are included in this amazing inheritance of truth-seeking. We recognize Jesus himself as the embodiment of truth for all of us.

PRACTICAL TIP: GOD'S CHARACTERISTICS IN YOU

Today, revisit the list you started in chapter four of God's characteristics. If you ask those who love you which characteristics most prevail in your life, which ones will they name? We may feel braggadocios to compare anything about ourselves to God's character, but he intentionally made us in his image (Genesis 1:26). It's okay to notice the tendency for his kids to look like him. In fact, we can take joy in looking like our heavenly Father, who is so good.

Take a minute to thank God for the way he designed you to reflect his personality, the beauty of his own Spirit. Depending on him to fill us with his Spirit unleashes our ability to reflect God's glory. Glorifying God is a lot like hanging a mirror on a wall behind a lamp. The mirror reflects the lamp's light, spreading beauty throughout the room. Like the mirror, we don't have to be the light ourselves—we are made to reflect God's beauty, goodness, and light.

MAY WE PRAY TOGETHER?

Dear heavenly Father, please notice us, your beloved children. Of course, we look like you, we are your children, after all. And yet, here we come again with our buckets empty. Teach us, O Lord, to understand that once we invite you into our lives, you never leave us but are our constant, faithful companion. Help us recognize your Spirit dwelling with us in our inner hearts. Teach us to present you first, instead of ourselves. Fill us with your presence so that all aspects of our hearts and all aspects of our lives honor you. Help us love truth so much we begin to reflect truth. Make us as much like your Son as humanly possible. Wash us with your living water. Let us overflow in joy to bless others. Bless us now because that's your heart's desire. In Jesus's name. Amen.

"Let your tongue speak what your heart thinks."
—Davy Crockett

CHAPTER 10:
OWN YOUR VOICE

HOW DOES WITHHOLDING TRUTH CHEAT THOSE AROUND US?

WE CAN SPEAK ASSERTIVELY BECAUSE OUR CONFIDENCE IS BASED ON HIS STATUS, NOT OURS.

> Jesus said to her, "I who speak to you am *He*." (John 4:26)

Personally, I am relieved I am not the savior of the whole world. Seriously, who has time for that? You'd have to give up your whole life and eat fewer potato chips. I'm not sure how potato chips made it into that last sentence except I was thinking of sacrifices. Potato chips immediately came to mind. Obviously, I am seriously under qualified for savior status if my mind can't even give up an imaginary bag of potato chips. Yes, the whole bag. Don't judge.

The woman at the well was a sympathetic blend of fear and faith, like all of us. Her mind was filled with questions based on her experience with prejudice and rejection. Simultaneously, she imagined and anticipated the Savior's arrival with pure faith.

She had a dilemma, though. *Should I trust him or not?* We can probably all relate.

We easily share our status—or lack of status—on Facebook, but when we bump up against controversial topics, we often shut down and withhold our perspective. Of course, withholding our opinions and feelings can be a healthy way to protect ourselves or practice patience with others. Withholding personal information about ourselves, however, can also be a way of building unhealthy, protective walls. In some extreme cases, withholding can even be a way of rejecting or a form of lying. As women, we often struggle to own our voice.

In this part of the passage, we see Jesus identify himself in the most vulnerable way, withholding nothing. He is taking a big chance here. Claiming to be the long-awaited Savior opens him up to all kinds of skepticism and ridicule by others, perhaps even being stoned to death. However, Jesus told her the truth anyway. In this one beautiful sentence, *I am he*, he invited the woman at the well to know him in the most vulnerable way by

- telling the intimate truth,
- inviting her into his sacred, and
- blessing her with mutual understanding.

TELLING THE INTIMATE TRUTH

The time had come to reveal a truly unique and intimate truth about himself. Once he shared his true identity, the pair could move from conversation to relationship.

Our culture has distorted the word *intimate*. We hardly recognize the term anymore. Yet, in this conversation, Jesus extended the clearest picture of who he is in the deepest recesses of his identity. Could anything be more sacred or intimate in a conversation?

The word sacred seldom finds its way into modern conversations. We're much more inclined to use the word intimate, another nuanced word. Yet, sacred beautifully describes the secret places of our inner person. When you look up the word sacred now the definition can seem diluted until it hardly holds any meaning at all. Because sacred is such an abstract concept, it's difficult to pin down. Some definitions suggest sacred as opposed to secular. We know sacred suggests a religious connection.

But God never intended us to trip over religion—he intended to seek us out for a relationship with him. Therefore, the sacred in our lives boils down to creating opportunity for relationship with him and others. For instance, our stories—even our past failures—become sacred when we tell them to invite others to connect with the loving, redeeming Savior.

Personally, I like synonyms to give us a better feel of what *sacred* means: blessed, divine, hallowed, holy, sanctified. Related words include sacrifice, sacrosanct, and sacrament. Clearly, this is a powerful word used to describe what is most holy and spiritual. Could there be a better word to describe the intimate stories of our hearts? When God's Spirit dwells with us in our inner person, could there be anything more sacred? Especially when he confirms our identity as his children and rewrites all our past, present, and future stories to honor him.

When the kind stranger arrived, she was prepared with good questions. It appears she'd occupied her mind with imagining the Savior for some time. She was ready, but she still challenged Jesus, holding him accountable to answer the hypocrisy of some religious leaders who misrepresented God. Based on their interaction so far, she felt ready to recognize the credibility of the claims he made. When Jesus told her the most intimate truth about himself, she believed.

Finally, the moment came when she understood her heart's desire had been answered. Against all odds, the Savior came to her well to talk to her, of all people. (Odd to her, but not to him. He sought her all along.) Perhaps, she'd been imagining this encounter for a long time. So, it wasn't that unexpected, was it? How could one woman have so much faith?

CRAZY IMAGINATION

Faith is often described for us in many ways, but here's one of my personal favorites from the author of Hebrews. "But without faith it is impossible to please Him, for he who comes to God must believe that He is, and that He is a rewarder of those who diligently seek Him" (Hebrews 11:6). Again, we encounter the power of imagination. Pondering the possibilities, no matter how seemingly crazy, is a key ingredient to faith.

Honestly, I doubt I would have the courage to look for him with such anticipation. Looking back at my own experience of coming to faith, I found it hard to believe the Savior wanted me, of all people. I am amazed at her insight to rely on God's countless promises in the Old Testament that a Savior would soon arrive.

Do you imagine deep conversations filled with wonderful authentic exchanges leading to better relationships and true companionship? If, in your craziest moments, you imagine some outrageous adventure involving pure influence, guess what? You are pre-qualified. Faith is the exciting adventure of imagining the possibilities and then trusting God for his beautiful plans. Your anticipation is evidence of faith. The time to own your voice is now.

For the woman at the well, he accomplished three things by telling her the intimate truth of who he is. He confirmed she was beloved and desirable for a relationship with him. He believed her companionship was worth seeking. He rewarded her anticipating faith with truth.

Like her, we are pre-qualified because he's been seeking us all along and inviting us into the most exciting adventure ever known to mankind: companionship with him. He invites us, too, to know his intimate truth. *I am He*, his Spirit whispers to our hearts.

INVITED INTO THE SACRED

The truth Jesus shares is so profound it will benefit anyone who will receive his message even today. In the words *I am He*, Jesus referenced one of the most famous verses in the Jewish Torah, or revered Book of the Law.

When Moses asked God for a name, God answered that his name is "I Am that I Am" (Exodus 3:14). Therefore, when Jesus asserted this same truth, the woman at the well understood the meaning. In responding to her mention of the Messiah,

Jesus chose words that could have easily incited a charge of blasphemy or even a riot in the woman's village.

He waited to speak this invaluable information until the perfect moment when her heart could embrace the truth for herself. Before her is the ruler of all, the focus of her faith, her hope of salvation. With confidence, he invited her to know him in the truest, most sacred way.

We can't imagine a scenario where he might withhold the truth from this woman who was so ready to know him. Yet, we are frequently tempted to withhold information, even in the face of great need. Exposing our most sacred stories to others can be costly. The risk requires us to be vulnerable. Thankfully, our truth is a lot less likely to incite a riot.

WE ARE WORTH SEEKING TOO

Like the woman at the well, we, too, must step into the relationship he offers. In a beautiful section of Paul's second letter to the Corinthians, he lovingly implores them to consider their true status of qualification: "Examine yourselves as to whether you are in the faith. Test yourselves. Do you not know that Jesus Christ is in you?—unless indeed you are disqualified" (2 Corinthians 13:5).

Through Paul's words, we have the opportunity to measure our own condition and consider if we really have God's Spirit living in our hearts. It's his presence in our spirits that qualifies us to be influential. Look at how plainly Jesus speaks of his own status. To understand our own status as his beloved children, we must be confident his Spirit dwells in our hearts.

In his bold statement, "I who speak to you am *He*," there can be no doubt of what Jesus is claiming. The woman already mentioned *Messiah*, another word for Savior. He is the One prepared to save the woman at the well, and in addition, each of us.

What does it mean to save someone? Sin and selfishness short-circuit all relationships, as we know. God took our sin upon himself because he cherishes a relationship with each of us.

Jesus was prepared to wipe out the debt created by sin. In fact, he came to Earth specifically seeking us to enter a relationship with him. He gave up his own unblemished life to free us from sin. Then, to prove he is ruler of everything, even death and sin, he was resurrected and enthroned again in heaven (Matthew 28:5–6). If he draws us to himself, as he did the woman at the well, he opens up eternal companionship with us now and in heaven.

Many of the coming events of Jesus's amazing work on Earth are still in the future. Yet, this Samaritan woman seizes the promise in this conversational moment. We can too. We have the advantage of hindsight she did not have. Jesus's work on the cross and his resurrection have happened. If Jesus had withheld the truth about his identity, this conversation would have been so much different for the woman at the well and for us. Instead, he spoke boldly.

As we think about owning our voice, I like what Jesus said about his voice in John 10:27: "My sheep hear My voice, and I know them, and they follow Me."

We, too, can learn to speak assertively, as we learn to trust Jesus's voice. He is a trustworthy shepherd, ever protecting and guiding us. Christians depend on God for his initiating, restorative relationship. That's a shout-worthy truth. We serve others when we speak up boldly about his goodness graciously offered to all and received by faith. On the one hand, habitually withholding truth can cause ongoing problems in relationships. On the other, speaking up boldly can become a healthy habit. A simple choice, but often so difficult to select.

SPEAKING UP WHEN IT COSTS YOU

Most people have struggled to speak up at one time or another. However, we must own our voice if we want to open our inner hearts to intimacy. Even if it feels like we get whipped up on or shunned when we finally do speak up. Is speaking up still worth it? Yes, of course. You've probably experienced similar situations, like the following examples.

In the last church meeting, Mike raised his hand, a rare event.

"If this building costs a million dollars, and we can only borrow a hundred thousand, how will we pay for the rest?"

Since the topic of the meeting was the latest building program, you would think his question might be well-received. Instead, silence communicated the group's frustration, now directed at him. He wanted to enlist everyone in a lively discussion of ways to raise funds, but his church's culture didn't include lively discussions. After the meeting, he felt discouraged and defeated. He began to pray for serious direction from God for his church. Fortunately, God hears our voice, even when others fail to listen.

Here's another example of how sharing truth can benefit others, even when it's hard to share. For Sally, the assault was the worst day of her life. She rarely spoke of it, even to her closest friends. Then, one day as she sat quietly between church services, a stranger sat next to her. The young woman seemed distressed and distracted. Almost before she knew what happened, Sally found herself sharing a small portion of her story to this complete stranger. Because she was willing to let down her guard, the young woman began to share her painful story too. Now, the young woman is plugged into a support group and well on her way to inner healing.

In another example, Nancy rehearsed all day how she would break the news to her new hubby. She dreaded going camping with his buddies, even though she was honored to be invited. She really wanted to stay home in their quiet apartment with no distractions, getting ahead on a project. No dirt, no smoky campfire, no public potties. Imagine her surprise when he looked relieved at her news. Thank goodness, she spoke kindly, but clearly. Everybody won because she did not withhold the truth from him. By owning her voice, she freed both of them to pursue a happy weekend and come back together refreshed.

We all have moments when we withhold truth because we think we might hurt the other person's feelings if we speak up. Perhaps we suspect the cost of telling the truth will be too high. Also, there are tender places in our hearts where we've been wounded, making us feel a need to protect ourselves. We may feel vulnerable to rejection, especially when sharing our perspectives or opinions in certain situations. It is so tempting to hide ourselves.

Of course, we should measure who we can trust and proceed judiciously, counting the cost against any potential benefit. However, if we have a habit of hiding, we need to look closely at that tendency. We want to free ourselves of any old bondages or false thinking. Each of us has something amazing to offer the world we live in. Sharing ourselves truthfully produces joy and influence when the time is right.

HIDING CHEATS OTHERS

Sometimes we fail to understand that withholding the truth cheats others. Like Mike's question about church finances, even a truthful question can get us ostracized. Often, like Sally, we may tend to withhold our story because vulnerability comes with real risk. I like the way Dana Goodrum explains feeling vulnerable, especially at church, in her book, *Open with Your Broken.* "So, anxiety creeps in when envisioning some picture-perfect museum of holy togetherness picking apart every piece of their flawed lifestyle, as they choose their seat in the very last row of the sanctuary, hoping to go unnoticed."[1]

The temptation to hide is real. Speaking out and boldly offering our perspective, even when our hearts tremble with fear of rejection, takes courage. Sadly, as Dana points out, church can be another place where we hide. The habit of hiding cheats others who may truly need to hear from us whether it's at home, at church, at work, or in our communities.

Plus, we also cheat ourselves out of the opportunity to be known and cherished for who we truly are.

FACING RISK IN OUR COMMUNITIES

How do we know when it's time to speak up with boldness? We do people no favors when we omit the truth or fail to speak up. There are times when intentionally withholding key information can have the same effect as lying. Many denominations call this a "sin of omission." There are also times when choosing to remain silent means we contribute to injustice.

"We can only make peace in a place where it's been compromised. Being a peacemaker will always entail risk," Ben Sciacca, author of *Meals from Mars*, explained when I interviewed him. "If I'm stepping out into a situation, a relationship, a context where peace has been violated or is vulnerable, that means I'm at risk; someone possibly getting angry with me or even possibly being hurt."

In everyone's life, speaking up sometimes means being brave and vulnerable, even forceful. Our communities are in desperate need of what we are called to say. Our conversations can combine gentleness with bold, assertive ideas.

"They call him the Prince of Peace. He entered a broken, dangerous world and allowed, actually allowed, that world to kill him so we can have a relationship. That's at the heart of peace-making. If he'd not taken that risk, it would be a different world today," Ben said.[2]

SHARING VITAL INFORMATION AT HOME

Making decisions to open ourselves up can be scary. Most of us fear rejection. We may even hedge our bets by only sharing the things other people easily accept.

I struggled to speak clearly with my husband early in my marriage. I preferred to avoid controversial topics, rather than risk an argument. Learning how to use healthy boundaries was a real challenge. I tended to go along without expressing my true opinions about our daily life.

For example, my husband's family loved to watch movies together late into the night at his parents' house, which was fun and snuggly as newlyweds. Then, when we had toddlers who needed to be at home in bed by 8:30, the habit became more difficult. I told all my close girlfriends about the problem. I told everyone, in fact, but David. We carried sleepy little ones to the car on many late nights, and I dealt with their grumpiness the next day. Eventually, I spoke up. By then, I was furious.

By withholding information, I had cheated David out of the opportunity to bless me and our kiddos. Plus, my anger splashed onto all my friends and eventually saturated my husband. What an unfair way to treat the people I love.

Likewise, failing to share basic information creates unnecessary problems. The fear of making certain situations worse may keep us silent. Some personality types are naturally more prone to caution, preferring peace at almost any cost. We can all freeze with unnecessary fear. However, opening ourselves up to others by speaking truthfully is foundational to creating relationships.

Additionally, withholding crucial information can be a kind of hypocrisy. Why? Because we give the impression we are more perfect or more spiritual than we actually are. Withholding vital information can be a symptom of people-pleasing. Therefore, we must find a way to loosen the grip of crippling ideas, even when they seem culturally acceptable.

To own our voice with gentle integrity is adventure at its finest. The risk of self-disclosure can be thrilling in a good way. With whole communities at stake, the risk is worth the sacrifice.

THE BLESSING OF MUTUAL UNDERSTANDING

Perhaps, we learned to clam up and play it safe as children. Speaking up doesn't mean we speak harshly. We can speak with boldness through tears if we speak with clarity.

For example, when I was about thirteen years old, my sister invited me to go to a Billy Graham movie. Billy Graham's face lit up the big screen as he encouraged me to accept Jesus as my Savior. I only wish I had accepted Jesus right then.

It wasn't an entirely futile night, though. Somehow, the movie dislodged a need buried deep in the recesses of my soul. Don't we all have a core need to feel loved?

Sobbing uncontrollably, I could barely breathe as I came into the den where my parents were waiting after the movie. Placing my hands on the dining table to steady myself, I prepared to tell my parents the "truth."

Imagine their panic. Had a young person died? Was I about to tell them I'd been hurt? Was I simply being melodramatic?

One of their biggest fears in the early seventies of my childhood was drugs—some things never change, I guess. My parents came over to the table and stood patiently with me as I caught my breath.

"I need ... *gasp* ... you ... *gasp* ... to say ... *gasp* ... 'I love you' to me more," I finally said between sobs.

Is that all? I'm pretty sure I sensed their relief. They hugged me and assured me they loved me. But would they get the message? Would they begin to speak their affection to me on a regular basis because I asked for what I needed?

Immediately, my mom began to frequently say, "I love you, Cathy." However, I soon recognized my dad found it extremely difficult to say those same words. I knew Dad loved me but saying so was another matter.

Like so many teenagers, I named a deep need. To my parents' credit, I trusted them. I knew, if I spoke the need, someone would try to meet it. I understood my dad's limits, even though it would be years before he developed the habit of telling me he loved me.

I'm not judging my dad for withholding vital information about his childhood from me when I was a child. In fact, I admire the way he eventually grew to share his most vulnerable, sacred stories at the appropriate time in my life.

In the meantime, he found other ways to express his affection without specifically saying, "I love you." By speaking assertively, through sobs, I opened up a new path for my relationship with my dad, even though it took years before new habits fully developed.

When it comes to sharing our personal stories, our earliest experiences may impact our ability to speak boldly. We may feel we've lost our voice. Perhaps we've been impacted by experiences we've almost forgotten, like the response of a parent or the teasing of neighborhood playmates.

As adults, we may need to offer others something we did not receive as children. To own our voice takes courage. We may even need to switch roles with parents to bless them as they age. Everyone benefits when we reclaim our childlike gift of speaking our personal truths clearly and with a humble heart.

FROM CONVERSATION TO RELATIONSHIP

What sets apart this conversation between Jesus and the Samaritan woman is they *both* shared their perspective. The truth shared between them allowed both spirits to connect with each other. The woman engaged at a deeply spiritual level with this gentle Son of Man because of the truth he offered about himself.

In this tender story, we see the transforming power of conversational adventures to create real relationship.

They have both faithfully and patiently spoken with boldness, without hiding, and now neither is cheated. He gave her no reason to hide as he expressed his love and respect for her throughout the conversation. Without fear, he clearly stated, *I am He.* His trustworthiness allowed her to recognize his true status as Savior.

Did he specifically seek her out by waiting for her at the well? Perhaps. But we don't know for sure. Certainly, she had been anticipating the arrival of the Messiah. Both claimed their mutual understanding and relationship together. They invited each other into a sacred relationship.

Her confidence is based on his identity. Keep reading because the best is still to come. In the next two chapters, we'll observe how she fulfills her own calling to influence. She extends Jesus's pure influence into her whole community and into our modern age thousands of years later. Plus, we'll catch a laugh at the humorous way this story comes to us down through the ages.

BEST QUESTION ABOUT ASSERTIVENESS

Assertiveness can easily be misconstrued as aggressiveness, so how do I know when to speak?

Being misjudged is a real risk when speaking assertively. However, we truly honor the other person when we present our perspective openly. When we own our voice, we invite the other person to know us as we truly are. Truth can be an unexpected gift.

When we own our voice, we often find ourselves laughing and rejoicing with others in community. We join in tender understanding of our own humanness and God's contrasting divinity.

Folks will reject us for our efforts at authenticity sometimes. This cannot be avoided. People will choose to reject the gentlest of help or the most vulnerable perspective. I suggest the 4-P Method. First, pause. Second, pray. Third, ponder. Finally, proceed judiciously. (In chapter eleven's Practical Tip, there's more on how to use the 4-P Method.)

We risk rejection when we speak assertively, of course, but we also offer respect, accountability, and companionship in our honesty. Truth holds us all accountable. Like Jesus and the woman at the well, when we share our sacred, we gain companionship forever.

We will see in the next chapter how credibility and humility are linked to influence. We'll also discover the disciples' own version of humor and joy in community and companionship. A habit of humor softens our assertive moments and brings balance to our lives. Stay tuned as Jesus's disciples show us how humor helps take the edge off our own foibles.

PRACTICAL TIP: ASSESS YOUR SPIRITUAL STATUS

Today, identify the state of your own spirit. Don't judge yourself. Don't add to your stress. Just tell yourself the truth. If necessary, comfort yourself the way you wish someone would offer comfort. Now, consider another possibility. Perhaps God himself would enjoy comforting you in the sacred places of your heart.

Rather than having a pity party, pick yourself up and dust yourself off. (Okay, I confess. I have pity parties. I try to limit myself to three days of whining and moaning. Then, I get back in the saddle and get out there.) Please own your beautiful spirit, even the broken pieces.

Even your hurting parts are beautiful because your spirit is a priceless treasure. By your spirit, you can enter into the presence of God's Spirit. What a truly remarkable miracle.

Allow yourself the dignity of cherishing him, worshiping him in spirit and truth. His identity and status as Savior forms the foundation of your confidence. Your ability to speak assertively with compassion hinges on his mercy and grace. If you have never begun a personal relationship with Jesus Christ, now is a perfect opportunity to invite the Savior into your life.

MAY WE PRAY TOGETHER?

Dear Father in heaven, you seek us out and we respond in our deepest spirits, where truth sometimes registers as pain. Whatever fear or wounds may live in our hearts, we are still your beloved children. We come to you now, desiring to worship you in spirit and truth. Help us combine humility with boldness, as we claim entrance into your presence by virtue of the cross on which Jesus died for us. Allow our hearts to honor and cherish you as we learn to be assertive in those special moments when it's necessary for your glory. Give us a voice to honor you. Help us to trust you when we speak truth, especially when a situation or relationship calls for peace-making. Thank you for giving us confidence in you, the Savior. Bless us now because that's your heart's desire. In Jesus's name. Amen.

"Courage is what it takes to stand up and speak; courage is also what it takes to sit down and listen."
—Winston Churchill

CHAPTER 11:
CLAIMING OUR CREDIBILITY

WHAT MAKES CERTAIN INFLUENTIAL PEOPLE SO CREDIBLE?
VULNERABLE HUMILITY.

> And at this point His disciples came, and they
> marveled that He talked with a woman; yet no one
> said, "What do You seek?" or, "Why are You talking
> with her?" The woman then left her water pot, went
> her way into the city, and said to the men, "Come,
> see a Man who told me all things that I ever did.
> Could this be the Christ?" Then they went out of
> the city and came to Him.
>
> In the meantime His disciples urged Him, saying,
> "Rabbi, eat." But He said to them, "I have food
> to eat of which you do not know." Therefore the
> disciples said to one another, "Has anyone brought
> Him anything to eat?" (John 4:27–33)

When a daughter falls in love, parents have a thousand
questions. What's he like? How does he treat his mother? Is
he worthy? Questions and worries crowd into our minds when
a daughter's heart is at stake. We might even try to head off
heartbreak from the moment the relationship begins. We really
have no choice but to pray on our knees in abject humility and
beg God to have mercy on us all.

Sometimes, the wonder of wonders happens, and the young
man turns out to be a worthy candidate for our daughter's love.

We fall on our knees, humbled before a God who answered our heart's most tender request in such a merciful way. Our concern melts to pure joy in anticipation of grandchildren and holidays spent in celebration. Let the fellowship begin!

Jesus helped the woman at the well understand her dream for companionship had come true. Here, in Samaria no less, was the true companion of her heart. We imagine both Jesus and the woman overflowing with joy, like a fountain of living water.

In this moment, a noteworthy shift happens. The newly claimed relationship shifts gears and the inclusion immediately spreads to others. We witness the woman's humility and eagerness to bring others to meet the Savior.

All along, Jesus sought her. He initiated one truth after another. She met his initiatives with imagination, assertiveness, and integrity. Now, the woman takes on the role of initiator. She invites all those in her community into the miracle taking place at their well.

Note another important and crucial strategy here: Jesus confirms his relationship with the woman by resisting pressure to cave to cultural prejudices. Remarkably, as he did so, the woman adopted several of Jesus's strategies for herself. She also extends inclusion to others by

- ignoring the cultural prejudices of the day,
- trusting pure instincts, and
- asking a good question.

IGNORING THE CULTURAL PREJUDICES OF THE DAY

Jesus focused his attention on a woman, despite the cultural prejudices of the day. His disciples were specifically intrigued by her status as a woman, "they marveled that He talked with a woman" (John 4:27). Yet, Jesus seemed unconcerned. As we know, he treated the woman with great respect, lavishing her with his undivided attention and intellect. I suspect the disciples learned a big lesson about their own prejudice as they observed how Jesus related to this woman.

Jesus's closest followers often rejoiced when others joined their ranks, much like parents who discover their daughter's bridegroom is worthy. In many cases, women encountered Jesus's respect for them, and their confidence blossomed as they followed him and cherished his leadership.

In this case, the disciples' cultural prejudice confused them for a moment. Then, later, they witnessed the radical change Jesus's conversation produced on a whole community. For the moment, Jesus's disciples seemed bemused and bewildered.

One of my favorite things about this passage is the way Jesus's credibility kept his disciples in check. We know what they were thinking because somebody wrote it down later. Otherwise, how would we know their thoughts? Clearly, they must have discussed the moment because they note they were all thinking the same thing. "And at this point His disciples came, and they marveled that He talked with a woman; yet no one said, 'What do You seek?' or, 'Why are You talking with her?'" (John 4:27).

I'm so amazed at the way they identified the cultural prejudices of the day. *What? Jesus is talking to a woman?* They marveled as their beloved Jesus boldly broke with tradition to do something so radically different. He is counterculture in this act. Yet, they did not speak up. Instead, they simply watched Jesus to see what would happen next.

Prejudice can leave us feeling bemused and bewildered too. Fortunately for us, Jesus gives us a terrific strategy for dealing with the prejudices of others. We can simply resist the pressure to cave in. We can include others.

Think about it this way. Marvel is the root word of marvelous. To be marvelous, sometimes we must put on our game face and let people marvel. There's something so stupefying about interacting with people in an unexpectedly loving way. Unexpected love and respect can cause people all around us to pause and pay attention. Naturally.

None of us expect other people to speak lovingly *and* assertively to us at the same time. What a rare combination. We can easily be taken off guard by such surprising behavior. And so will those you're seeking to engage.

THE WELL

Unexpected Invitations to Converse

I'll share an example that really exposes my age. Like me, you may remember when dying hair bright peacock blue was an unexpected fashion statement for young people. Blue hair sent shivers down the spine of old folks. *Was this rebellion afoot? What did these new fashion statements mean?* Old people like me simply couldn't compute the message. In my day, blue hair was for grannies who misjudged the amount of dye to use in their hair.

"I see you have blue hair," I blurted to the young man standing in front of me at the movies one Friday night. His eyes squinted, giving away his expectation. He set his jaw, ready to defend his fashion choice, every muscle tense.

"I figure if you do something out of the ordinary, you're inviting comments," I said. "I try to respond whenever I see folks starting a conversation with their fashion. I just want you to know I see you."

A huge smile lit his face. Once he got over his shock at my boldness, we had a really nice conversation, filled with a few laughs about our divergent perspectives about fashion. (I've been wearing rhinestones and leopard print leggings since the eighties, so I really have no room to judge.)

I've learned people do seemingly crazy stuff to start up conversations. Tattoos are the same way. People love to share the sacred stories connected to their skin art. A small break with traditional courtesy—blurting out the seemingly impolite comment—sometimes yields a treasure load of adventurous conversation.

To be people of influence, we must take risks in starting conversations with humility, shaking off any preconceived ideas that hold us back.

Cultural Prejudices Hold Us Back

Often, cultural prejudices keep us tied to unhealthy ways of looking at life. If only we could shake off all the labels.

Labels, like racism, stop progress in its tracks. In east Texas, people still subconsciously self-segregate along racial lines. Obviously, work and school bring people from all ethnicities together, but, unfortunately, Sunday morning church services are often a different story.

In 1960, Martin Luther King, Jr. said, "I think it is one of the tragedies of our nation, one of the shameful tragedies, that eleven o'clock on Sunday morning is one of the most segregated hours, if not the most segregated hours, in Christian America."[1] In east Texas, there's still a lot of truth to his observation. For many reasons, not every church, but many, still tend to divide along racial lines.

Fortunately, churches are gradually attempting to shake off these cultural prejudices and finding ways to pull down the entrenched racial barriers in our region. Progress is made each Sunday as courageous people cross traditional cultural barriers to claim unity. It's slow going, though. The way we talk about the race gap makes it more difficult to cross. If only we chose words which could create freedom and room for growth.

PREJUDICE OR BIASED RACISM?

I miss the word *prejudice*, for instance. We heard that word all the time in the sixties and seventies. The word often implied someone had an irrational antipathy toward people of another ethnic background. In fact, we all suffer from preconceived ideas. The word prejudice has been replaced by more sinister words today. People commonly use the term *racism* or *racist* now. *Biased* is another common term. Words matter, and here's a great example of why. The words racist or biased convey a finite, permanent label, as if change is impossible.

In contrast, the word *prejudice* means to pre-judge, implying an assessment is made without enough information. Therefore, add education and the assessment can be reexamined for a more judicious conclusion. Prejudice, by its definition, can change to enlightenment with the addition of knowledge and wisdom.

Prejudice is closely related to the word judicious, sharing the root idea of judgment. Unlike prejudice, the word *judicious* conveys the idea people can ponder, absorb new information, and, therefore, live wisely.

THE WELL

The disciples experienced confusion because of their cultural prejudice about the status of women. To their credit, rather than locking into a bias, we know they began to process a new perception. They later recorded their perspective change with self-effacing humor and insight for us. In fact, their humorous account of the events sheds light on how humble Jesus's disciples really were.

The writers of this account chose to leave out the details of the woman's story, but I suspect the disciples grew to respect and cherish her as their Savior did. Perhaps the gaps that make this story so intriguing were intentional. Rather than rehash an old, promiscuous past, they may have deleted details out of respect for her. Or, perhaps, they simply realized the story was about him, not her.

Whatever the case, their clever telling of the events draws us in. With a wink at their own confusion, they share how befuddled they were. I picture them bumbling around like the three stooges. Who brought him dinner? What bread? How did he get food we don't know about? It might be easy to miss the humor here if we've never seen Abbott and Costello's Who's on First gag.

I imagine the disciples laughing about their confusion later around a campfire. Don't ask me why I always imagine the disciples around a campfire, but I do. What amazes me most, though, is how they included this part of the story in their written account, as if inviting us to laugh with them. What a beautiful example of how humility and self-effacing humor are related.

Their prejudice about her status as a woman melted away in light of her joyful understanding and actions. Plus, I suspect Jesus's obvious devotion contributed to their respectful treatment of her in this account.

Oh, to be like Jesus, simply free to ignore other people's bewilderment as we go about our lives in companionship and peace. And to be like the disciples, able to laugh later about our silly ideas.

The disciples don't question Jesus's reasoning for doing something so out of the ordinary for their culture. They simply

170

trust him. They know from experience he will explain later, if necessary. His credibility and integrity are palpable in the way his disciples remain silent as their own prejudice is challenged.

BRAVE AND NOBLE

We know the disciples got the message because of the way they later recorded this account. As far as we know, Jesus never addressed their concerns at all. His actions toward the woman communicated enough. He felt no need to grab a teaching opportunity to talk about the valued status of women. Even in his resting, Jesus's conversation with the woman communicated brave and noble ideas.

Notably for us, there are two primary ways we teach our children to be brave and noble: through words or through actions. Sometimes a combination of both is imperative. When we combine brave and noble ideas with actions and words, even resting mode becomes a powerful method for conveying truth to our kids.

I still believe in the power of well-chosen words to drive home truth—telling a story or picking up a handy visual aid. But oh, how glorious for a young parent to give yourself a break and simply rest.

Unchaining ourselves from unhealthy prejudices takes fortitude and integrity. There are plenty of times with our children when doing something out of the ordinary—something brave and noble—frees them to grasp truth. Fortunately, though, having done the hard work, we don't always have to talk about it afterwards. Those courageous moments don't require any extra explanation.

As a parent, I was relieved to discover my kiddos could process information just fine without my help and often did, thank you very much! What a blessing to rest and trust God's Spirit to reveal truth to them in their own hearts.

For some, looking to Jesus is the best healing option when it comes to parenting our children to be brave and noble. For others, we can look to our own earthly fathers for hints. Either way, whether you're raising sons or daughters, Rick Johnson offers powerful advice in his book *Better Dads, Stronger Sons*.

"Try to remember the good things your dad taught you and pass those on to your son. That kind of modeling is the way adult males have always taught boys to become men. It's not the telling as much as the doing."[2]

Often, life requires us to take the brave stand. We are called to do the bold and unexpected. Rest mode allows us to just *be*. Be kind. Refuse to limit yourself. Choose to cross self-segregating lines. Offer friendship. Be vulnerable and open. Get out of the fast lane and make time for your family. All these things are courageous acts and we can do them in resting mode.

There's something so beautiful and persuasive about a courageous life lived with intention and vulnerability, minus the fanfare.

Now, Jesus takes a deep breath and seizes advantage of a quiet moment to speak to his disciples. As he does so, the woman proceeds to claim the influence God has already prepared for her. She moves to include others as this amazing story unfolds. Ah, the beauty of action, inclusion, rest, teaching, and influence all combined.

TRUSTING PURE INSTINCTS TO INCLUDE OTHERS

The woman confirmed her ready status by taking immediate action. She instantly did the most credible thing anyone could think of—she went directly to the most trusted leaders in her community and included them in the news.

Just think, wonder of wonders! The most unexpected surprise ever known in this little village is happening before her eyes. The Savior of the world is in Samaria, of all places. Clearly, she did not miss the point.

Her instincts were pure gold. She was in such a hurry she didn't even bother to carry her water pot with her. Imagine how Jesus must have noted her quick action. Did her enthusiasm comfort his heart and energize his weariness? Maybe she left the water pot for her new friend and his disciples since she was coming right back anyway.

Her enthusiastic response reminds me of a young man proposing to his intended. With bated breath, he wonders if he's won her heart. If he's wise, he gets her dad's approval ahead of time. He kneels before his sweetheart with a trembling heart. The young groom-to-be hopes he will soon present her to all his loved ones as his fiancée and, then, as his wife.

Observing young couples in love gives us only a dim image of the exuberant, celebratory love God has for us. In fact, his Son is called the bridegroom (John 3:29). There is no better companion than Jesus if we want to experience a lifetime of sacrificial, devoted love.

Come See!

Filled with excitement, the woman dashes off to influence her whole community. I can easily imagine Jesus taking a deep breath and smiling with satisfaction. He rested as his disciples tended to him. His greatest desire was already in motion. Having shared his most sacred truth, *I am He*, he now has the pleasure of seeing her response.

We hold our breath as the drama comes to a crescendo in this captivating story. We could easily write the script for the television teaser for the next episode. How will her newfound passion play out? Can she hide from her past? Will her community leaders respond to her or reject her message?

Jesus may be taking a breather, but the story is moving ahead in high drama. This woman now adopts a couple of Jesus's own strategies for appealing to her community's leaders: 1. sharing her own sacred story, and 2. asking a good question. She brings an invitation to her leaders.

Sharing Sacred Stories Takes Courage and Commitment

First, with her invitation, she honestly acknowledges and owns her own past—her sacred story reexamined by her Savior. Her courage and commitment are expressed in humility. She starts the new conversation from a position of truthfulness and vulnerability to reach the people she loves.

"Come, see a Man who told me all things that I ever did" (John 4:29).

As she opens her past up for examination, she places her confidence in Jesus alone. She calls him, "the Man who told me all things that I ever did."

On one hand, if her community ostracized her due to her own misbehavior, her statement may have been a direct challenge to community leaders. She might be communicating one truth. *He approves of me and accepts me—what do you say about that?* On the other hand, if she was a respected community servant, perhaps she is simply glad he gave her credit for serving others. Either way, she is surely surprised a stranger would know so much about her life.

We don't necessarily think of assertiveness and gentleness together and yet, in effective communication, they are closely related. The woman at the well demonstrated a beautiful example of how humility sets up the opportunity to assert truth. With grace, she cuts through any objections her neighbors might harbor about her or her reputation in one quick sentence.

In addition, by being so humble about all she'd ever done, she also acknowledges Jesus's uncanny, even supernatural, knowledge of her history. Instead of claiming her own credibility, she references his credibility as truth teller. What beautiful foreshadowing of the astonishing truth she is about to reveal. She also shifts the responsibility to her community—it's up to them to decide if they believe her when she presents his identity as the Savior.

Will they come? Will they consider her question? This remarkable woman opens a conversation with her community leaders by setting aside any false pretensions. With deferential respect, she displays a powerful, robust testimony. She desires to speak truth and her tenderhearted approach opens the opportunity.

She immediately draws others to join her in the conversational adventure she has been having with the Savior. How does she accomplish so much, so quickly? By asking a good question.

Asking a Good Question

To me, the second part of what she does is even more informative than the first part. Opening up her past for examination is amazing, but she also exercised one of Jesus's most effective strategies—she asked a good question. "Could this be the Christ?"

We really can't overlook how much like Jesus she becomes in this moment. In their book, *Power Questions*, Andrew Sobel and Jerold Panas explain the significance of a good question in the earlier interaction of Jesus and the woman.

"The encounter, which Jesus starts with the question, 'Will you give me a drink?' transforms her."[3] Questions are so powerful, Jesus begins with one, as does the woman at the well with her community's leaders.

In contrast, nothing stops conversation like an emphatic statement which broaches no discussion. How many times have I blurted out my opinion, leaving no room for anyone else's? Whether it's a lecture with our kids or a scolding to our spouse, nothing ruins conversation like dogmatic opinion, disguised as truth-telling. Opening with a simple question is always better.

"Could this be the Christ?" With her question, she avoids any argument, which might have resulted if she stated emphatically the Savior was at their well. She resists the temptation to tell them exactly what she suspects. What a woman! I admire her fortitude.

Did she respect their freedom to decide for themselves? Is that why she asked, rather than told? Possibly. Perhaps, she still sought truth herself. Did she want the confirmation of trustworthy leaders as she came to her own conclusion? This could have been one of those times when a double check by trusted people seemed like a good idea. The situation certainly seemed too good to be true. The Savior? At *our* well?

By engaging their imagination with her question, she avoids any distracting, doctrinal disputes. Additionally, she manages to hold them accountable with the truth. She frees them to respond with enthusiasm. Thankfully, for them and us, they respond in an instant. "Then, they went out of the city and came to him" (John 4:30). As we will see in the next chapter, many believed because of her testimony.

Meanwhile, Back at the Well, Some Pretty Funny Stuff

In contrast, the disciples seem confused and distracted. Preoccupied with their daily tasks, they wonder about all the wrong stuff.

You can almost hear the disciples chuckling as they write the account. It reminds me of hilarious friends who often mishear conversations to everyone's entertainment. One person asks, "What do you want for dinner?" and the other person answers, "Why would I want to be thinner?" Say, what?

What a sense of humor and high drama. In telling the account of what happened, the disciples humbly share their confusion about all the wrong things as a comical part of the story.

Like the disciples, it's easy to be distracted in the exhaustion of daily chores and responsibilities. Who hasn't been distracted while fixing supper? Or missed a sweet moment with a toddler while washing a pile of laundry?

We get so preoccupied with daily life, we blink and miss our own crucial moments. My children still laugh about the time I got called into their elementary school principal's office.

"Cathy, did you know Anna came to school yesterday in her socks with no shoes?"

I scrunched my shoeless feet under my chair and placed my big purse in front of them. I usually keep an extra pair of tennis shoes in my car, but Anna wore my shoes into school that day.

"Um, yes. Our shoes stay by the back door, and we keep forgetting to bring them with us in the car. You know, as we're grabbing all the lunchboxes and backpacks."

"This is not the first time it's happened. Try to do better."

"Yes, ma'am."

In the stress of the day, we can easily miss life's most beautiful moments. Often, our moments of human foibles become hilarious stories later. How kind and encouraging of the disciples to share the humor in their humanness. We're in excellent company.

Like the disciples, humility frees us to laugh at ourselves and enjoy life. I've wasted too much of my life worrying ahead or regretting the past. Even uncomfortable moments can morph into merriment later, like Mommy getting pulled into the principal's office without her shoes.

In the next chapter, we'll see how Jesus identifies his own most pressing need. Did you ever think about Jesus as needing anything? Together, we'll examine his profound insights about togetherness and joy. As we come to the end of this conversational adventure, we can't help but savor the contrast from the opening scene when the woman at the well arrived alone. As we conclude, we'll witness a whole community brought together around the Savior because of her heart's ready response to him. Oh, to be that person in our communities.

Best Question about Vulnerability

What if, while being truly vulnerable, I feel I have no credibility to offer others?

First and most importantly, we are not dependent on our own accomplishments or experiences to be credible and qualified. Credibility hinges on sharing truth with humility. Seeking truth is a sure way to find it, as Jesus promised (John 17:1–24). In fact, he promises to reward truth-seekers. We must wonder if the woman at the well met him for one simple reason. She sought truth and he honored his promise to reward those who seek. He is the truth she sought. Truth found her.

When you seek him with a humble heart, he qualifies you for his purpose in your life. God's will for us is simple. He desires for us to become more and more like Jesus. A wonderful description of God's will in Thessalonians 5:8 includes rejoicing, praying, and giving thanks. It's easy to imagine Jesus exemplifying all these.

Additionally, you are probably more gifted than you realize. Perhaps, like Eve, the devil already has his eye on you because you seek truth and desire wisdom. Without fear, seek truth where it can be found—in a relationship with the Savior. Embrace your giftedness, especially if the gift is a relationship with Jesus. Our credibility hinges on our readiness to acknowledge him.

We all have experience, skills, talents, and reputations to put on a résumé. Unlike résumés, however, sometimes our frailties and mistakes speak most powerfully to others. As we share our stories in humble and vulnerable ways, we discover others who respond.

Like the woman at the well, we can learn to live humbly, opening our stories up for others to examine. We can focus attention on Jesus's credibility as we acknowledge his place in our lives. His status as Christ, the Savior, is all that matters. In our humility and weakness, his profound love is amplified.

PRACTICAL TIP: FLEX YOUR CREDIBILITY BY PONDERING WISELY

As you review your day, consider the needs of those you met. Perhaps a coworker seemed especially needy. Maybe one of your children truly needed a little tough love today. Add any plumbing issues or deadlines and you have a recipe for exhaustion. I don't know about you, but it wears me right out thinking about all the stuff happening on any given day in my world.

First, give yourself permission to pause. Forego taking any action at all for a while. Now, you can take the time you need to pray as you ponder on the needs of others. Prayer is no small gift to give to others or ourselves. Through prayer, we access wisdom from the One who is fully present, divinely compassionate, and completely authentic. We draw deeply from his well of loving kindness for us through prayer.

Having thoughtfully turned to him for wisdom, it may be time to proceed with an action he prescribes. With his wisdom, we can proceed when we feel called to act on others' behalf.

Thus, you can use the 4-P Method—Pause, Pray, Ponder, Proceed—especially whenever negative emotions catch you off guard.

True credibility relies on Jesus's status, not our own. In this world, among our family and friends, our credibility develops over time. We offer others a chance to know the Savior as we get to know him too. The woman deferred to others, even as she invited them to meet the Savior. We must respect others' right to see for themselves too.

May We Pray Together?

Dear Father in heaven, your Son alone is the Savior. Sometimes, we think we are more responsible than we are. We fumble and acutely feel our inadequacies. Today, help us remember to seek the truth that you offer. You promise to make holy all who seek you (John 17:17–23). The only credibility we need is yours. We humbly ask you to give us courage to be vulnerable and open. For true companionship with you, we are grateful. Teach us to seek your wisdom to benefit others. None of our accomplishments qualify us, and our past does not disqualify us. Give us joy overflowing as we rest in your beautiful Holy Spirit, the living water who drenches the human soul with love. Bless this one now because that's your heart's desire. In Jesus's name. Amen.

"Humor is mankind's greatest blessing." —Mark Twain

CHAPTER 12:
TRUTH SEEKERS

WILL I EVER GET THE CREDIT I DESERVE?
YES, BY CULTIVATING JOY AND COMMUNITY.

> *And many of the Samaritans of that city believed in Him because of the word of the woman who testified, "He told me all that I ever did." So when the Samaritans had come to Him, they urged him to stay with them; and He stayed there two days. And many more believed because of His own word.*
>
> *Then they said to the woman, "Now we believe, not because of what you said, for we ourselves have heard Him and we know that this is indeed the Christ, the Savior of the world." (John 4:39–42)*

A troupe of cultural exchange performers from Ariel, Israel danced, sang, and laughed their way into our hearts a while back. Ariel is a small town near Jacob's well in Israel, the actual well where this story took place.

The students from Ariel and their leaders entertained us with joy and camaraderie. I visualize the community leaders in this biblical passage as never before because of these new friends.

These young Israelis reveled in the history of their country. They joyfully shared insight with us, answering all questions asked in typical blunt Texas fashion. They were united in their perceptiveness and their sense of humor. When I think of the leaders brought to Jesus by the woman at the well, I see the different faces of these good modern-day men and women, smiling with joy, curiosity, and love.

Jesus offered rejoicing as a byproduct of joining him in God's purpose. He affirmed the woman's influence and credibility. We'll see how her story comes to us as a credit to her beautiful heart.

Do any of us ever get the credit we deserve? Eventually, we know we'll receive the delight of spending eternity with Jesus in heaven. Are there earthly rewards in the meantime? Yes, like Jesus, we can cultivate joy and community, too. Just look how Jesus fostered joy and fellowship by

- rejoicing together,
- extending his presence, and
- staying to seal the deal.

REJOICING TOGETHER OR, UM, FEELING GUILTY

Jesus's disciples gave this woman credit for the new faith of her community leaders and many who came with her. Ironically, the Samaritans themselves did not. Some of the Samaritans tell her it's not because of what she said that they believe. Could both accounts be true? Yes, and there's some humor in the telling. Best of all, the town's people claimed their faith due to spending time with Jesus for themselves. They honored this stranger who came to them, calling Jesus the Christ and Savior of the world.

First, let's look at how Jesus linked rejoicing and togetherness. As the woman scooted off to share her news, he turned to his disciples and lavished truth on them. Between verses 33 and 39, Jesus shares with his disciples, perhaps to prep them for what is about to happen. He emphasized the time to work will come to an end. We receive the pleasure of listening in on his teaching. "Jesus said to them, My food is to do the will of Him who sent Me, and to finish His work. Do you not say, "There are still four months and *then* comes the harvest'? Behold, I say to you, lift up your eyes and look at the fields, for they are already white for harvest! And he who reaps receives wages, and gathers fruit for eternal life, that both he who sows and he who reaps may rejoice together. For in this the saying is true: "One sows and another reaps." I sent you to reap that for which you have not labored; others have labored, and you have entered into their labors."' (John 4:34–38)

I don't know about you, but over the years I've felt guilty when I've read this passage. Am I doing enough? I carefully manage my schedule with healthy boundaries, as modern people do, but still. Couldn't I be doing more for the kingdom? Do you check your calendar and put things off to next month, like I do, to make room for other priorities?

What about the opportunities I miss because I keep such a demanding schedule? How do I measure my priorities with confidence? As Jesus begins to teach his disciples, he speaks to the procrastinator in me. *How did he know?*

"Do not say, 'There are still four months ...'" (John 4:35). Oh, my goodness, it's as if he reached through time to speak to me via this story, like he's sitting right next to me, looking at my packed calendar. My mind flashes to the important conversations I've failed to have with family and friends who don't know him. Sharing Jesus is the single most life-changing conversational adventure we can have, and yet, I seem to find a million other superficial things to talk about instead.

I suspect my self-condemning, guilty conscience previously kept me from grasping Jesus's point—and I wrote a whole chapter on false guilt. It's like Jesus gives a half-time pep talk and I still feel guilty about the interception I caused in the first quarter. (I know, a football analogy from me, of all people.) I think what he's telling his disciples, and us, is to shake off any distractions, like, ahem, false guilt, and check back into reality. Now is the time for the win. However, we must do it together as a team. How do we tackle distractions and go for the goal of joy?

THE JOY OF NOT DOING IT ALL

Rejoicing and togetherness go hand in hand. Fortunately, Jesus knows our over-achieving, foolish ways of thinking.

THE WELL

Did we suppose rugged individualism was an invention of American cinema courtesy of John Wayne? I like John Wayne movies as much as anyone else, but our human tendency to think *it's all up to me* is nothing new. Responsible people, who bless lots of folks with their service, often tend to take on more responsibility than is rightfully theirs. We cheat ourselves of the joy of collaboration when we overreach our responsibilities.

There are at least three tasks described here: planting, cutting, and gathering. For those of us who live in the country, harvest always involves lots of people and lots of equipment, especially tractors. I couldn't resist throwing tractors in here because when it comes to harvesting, Texas guys love their tractors. Some men buy land just as an excuse to buy a tractor. I am not kidding.

In modern times, planting or sowing starts with preparing the soil and choosing the right seeds. Both parts involve teams of experts. There are stores called feed stores, where they sell food for farm animals and tons of additives to correct soil issues. Plus, there are stores that sell nothing but tractors and special attachments for tractors. (See how I worked in the word tractor again? If you're reading this out loud to your husband, you can thank me later.)

Cutting, or reaping, again involves lots of people, sometimes whole teams of subcontractors to help the farmer cut or pick the crop.

Gathering the fruit refers to any crop, not just fruit like pineapples or strawberries. Gathering in the harvest requires tractor attachments specially designed to gather specific crops. There's a special set of attachments and trucks to gather cotton, for example. Cotton is a common crop in the fields around Waco and many parts of Texas. Harvesting cotton is a grand production each year.

Whether they produce on small farms like many of the rose-growers where I live or cultivate hundreds of acres like many cotton growers, farmers today understand Jesus's analogy in this passage. Farmers understand the harvest is a team effort.

Why would we waste a minute feeling guilty about jobs designed to be shared with others? Me and my silly false guilt. What a waste of energy. If Jesus came to seek us for companionship with God in eternity, naturally, he would design a process that meant companionship in this world too.

Rejoicing Together: Jesus's Highest Priority

What if I told you the greatest joy in life is getting together with friends to bring others to God? It could be the thing Jesus most loves and "needs." Remember, he was seeking companionship as he sat at the well and asked the woman for a drink. In verse 33, he told his disciples "I have food to eat of which you do not know." What food did he mean?

It's hard to consider the Savior of the world needing anything, even food. Yet I suspect Jesus identifies his own most pressing need in these verses. Again, using a handy visual aid—food—he clarifies his most pressing need and his greatest pleasure. He says his *food* is to do the will of God and finish the work begun by God. What a fascinating claim of heartfelt unity with God the Father.

As Jesus invites us to share his joy, he reveals what he most desires, or *needs*. He invites the woman, his disciples, the Samaritans, us, all who will come, to join him in unity with his Father. Joy is designed to be shared. Together, let's examine Jesus's profound insights about togetherness and joy.

Jesus says, "both he who sows and he who reaps may rejoice together" (John 4:36). He describes this harvest-producing process as a source of togetherness and joy. If Jesus looks forward to the harvest with anticipation, how much more can we anticipate joy as we join in with him?

What is this harvest? Harvest is simply the beautiful process of inviting others to join us as we share the sacrificial love and tenderness of the Savior of the world. Ah, the sweetest form of companionship to ever exist.

To harvest, we join the process of cultivating companionship as we share his message. The process follows a pattern similar to farmers cultivating crops. We enlist help. We offer seedling ideas, we water, fertilize, watch for growth, invite others to enjoy the fruit of our labors, and, when the time is right, we come together to enjoy the rich blessings of abundance.

When harvesting for the kingdom, the harvest may be a movement across our nation of new loving unity with a spirit of justice and mercy. Or the harvest could be as simple as trying something new in our own little family to teach our children how to love with tenderness and wisdom.

For harvest to bear fruit—the most important thing to note about Jesus's words—we must work and celebrate together with joy. My beloved reader and friend, we are invited to the greatest, most fun party ever. The delightful celebration of a Savior who includes us in his conversational adventures. We've reached the most beautiful truth about influence. It happens together with joy.

EXTENDING HIS PRESENCE: THE SAVIOR IS HERE! AT OUR WELL!

Jesus mentioned the sowing, or seed planting, has already taken place because the harvest is ready. Often, teachers say this includes the prophets who preceded Jesus, predicting his arrival. I also wonder if the woman at the well ran to tell her community leaders about the Savior because someone in her community predicted his imminent arrival. Had a rabbi or community leader been teaching the prophesied Christ could come any day?

Perhaps the woman watched for the Savior because one of the leaders had been teaching the community to be alert for the Savior's coming. Thus, she sought a specific leader. Was she prepared because the leaders of the community were united in anticipating his arrival? I like to think so. I imagine her seeking a revered teacher and his friends to let him know his dream of a Savior could now be reality. *Come quickly to meet him! Could the Savior be here? At our well!*

Did Jesus wait at the well aware the woman would soon return with others, perhaps including a beloved teacher or mentor? In the interim, he spoke to his disciples about being closers. Those who reap and those who gather are both functions of the closing stage of harvest—cutting the crop and gathering it up.

The disciples were about to witness a whole community gathered to meet Jesus. Perhaps he was planting seeds in the disciples' hearts. Maybe Jesus made them aware so they wouldn't miss the unfolding drama. What they needed to understand about spiritual harvesting was about to transpire before them. Spiritual harvesting is a perfect picture of how influence is designed by God to work in our lives, our families, our churches, and our communities.

Like harvesting fruit, many times we need to close in on inviting people to join in community. We extend his presence and influence by inviting people to come and know Jesus. We really cheat ourselves when we are too timid to be closers. Why not ask the risky questions about faith?

Joy is the byproduct of a relationship with him and others. Joy is multiplied when we join together. There is no greater joy than sharing in the moment when another person decides to invite Jesus into their life. Could there be any better joy in life than to share such an adventure with someone we love?

We've raised a couple of kids we call closers. David and I always joked they had a future in sales. Perhaps you, too, are raising confident kids who know how to ask for what they want. Saying no to closers can be trying for parents. Sure enough, though, those personality traits can be a true blessing as they become adults. Closers go about their day zooming in on ways to meet others' needs.

Obviously, no one wants to be manipulated into making a bad purchase by someone who knows how to close a deal. The best closings happen when everyone loves the deal that's made. What we say in our family is, "When God is in it, everybody gets a blessing." A great example of making a good deal for everyone came when my mom was ready to sell our family home.

As Mom made the decision to move in with us, we looked for any creative ways to rezone or reprocess her house. The house had great "bones," but also needed plenty of rehab.

In the end, we prayed for a young family who wanted square footage but didn't mind investing some sweat equity. When the closing happened, everyone received a blessing. The buyer got a lot of house for the money. Mom felt terrific selling to a young family who would create memories in the home she'd loved for almost fifty years. My siblings and I were happy to turn the rehab over to anyone else.

We can enjoy a dream for a while, then hand it off to future dreamers, much like Mom loved turning her home over to a new young family. Other times, we join in at the end simply to bring a project to completion. Rarely do we see a vision from beginning to end. Many people join in along the way whenever a vision becomes reality, much like an abundant harvest.

Jesus invites us to faithfully till the soil and plant seeds in season as we go along. All around us people are ready to hear the message Jesus brought of loving companionship with God. We can join others to reap when the harvest is ready. Then, we gather each other together to rejoice, including those who are new to the faith.

How does this look in our modern times? We cultivate friendships with others. Together, we share testimonies and spiritual truths. All along the way, we seek to include others, respecting their free will. As a habit, we embrace humility, speaking truth with tenderness. We own our voice. Together, we reject envy and prejudice, accepting others with empathy and compassion. We seek peace, rather than arguments. With courage, we take on tough topics, always keeping the well-being of others at heart. Like Jesus, we rest.

Jesus's people need to love him together. Without false guilt, after we've worked diligently, we can look at the fruitfulness of our lives and rejoice. Thus, we secure the spiritual well-being of our families and friends. This creates the balance of work, rest, joy, and community seen demonstrated by Jesus in this beautiful account.

COMMUNITY LEADERSHIP

Traditionally, some have taught that the woman blackmailed the community leaders with their own sordid pasts—perhaps even involving her. Thus, she forced them to acquiesce to her request for attention in this moment. Perhaps these men felt shame for their culpability and were afraid to ignore her, according to such interpretations.

I find this illogical based on what we know about human nature. Any person with a guilty conscience will try to avoid public scrutiny. We will even make self-righteous comments rather than admit we've sinned.

When ashamed, we tend to withdraw and hide. We see it in the garden when Adam and Eve hid from God (Genesis 3:8), and we still see it today. Sure, some people cheat and get away with it for a while, but leaders who are guilty of being unfaithful seldom stand amidst the scrutiny of community.

However, this dear woman was well-received when she fearlessly approached the men of her community. At her request, community leaders showed up curious, open, and eager to meet the stranger at the well. Rather than hiding, making excuses, or slinking off, these leaders boldly walked into an unpredictable conversational adventure with a man claiming to be the Savior. Based on the woman's testimony alone, they rushed to meet Jesus.

Along the way, others joined them as word spread of the stranger's possible identity. Is it any wonder the woman at the well becomes known throughout the centuries for her beautiful lingering conversation with Jesus, followed by the way she enthusiastically influenced a whole community? Her response to his message secured opportunity for spiritual well-being for herself. Her quick desire to share the living water she received meant the invitation to know him rippled out. All who join her in responding, meet him as well.

JESUS STAYS TO SEAL THE DEAL

Word sure spreads fast in a small town. Although she originally went to the community leaders, a whole crowd of Samaritans also gathered to meet the stranger. If Texas is any indication, any excuse will do for a gathering in a small town. Jacksonville has the Tomato Fest, Athens has their

Black-Eyed Pea Festival, and Ben Wheeler has a Feral Hog Festival complete with plastic pink snouts on elastic. And that's just within a few miles of my house.

As the community gathered around the well, we're reminded of Jesus's words about the gathering of a fruitful harvest. Jesus already said he was not talking about literal fruits and veggies (or tomatoes, peas, or pork). Fruit gathering is about "fruit for eternal life." Now, as the crowd gathered and the disciples looked on, Jesus demonstrated what it meant to gather fruit for eternal harvest.

The Scriptures tell us that the Samaritans "urged him to stay with them" (John 4:40). He responded by remaining in their town for a time. Often, we must plant our feet and commit ourselves to staying to create the kind of companionship we want. Time translates as affection in all our relationships. Jesus affirms the significance of all the Samaritans by staying with them.

That phrase, "urged him to stay," brings tears to my eyes. Imagine having a Savior who stays with us, too, simply because we urge him.

Jesus also affirmed the credibility of this influential woman by staying on two additional days. He sought her out. She trusted him to be true. Now, he honors her by being exactly who she believed him to be.

BECAUSE OF HIS OWN WORD

At first glance, we might feel a little shortchanged. Perhaps it feels like we don't get enough information to listen in on their two-day conversation. It's like being invited to the biggest, best ladies' conference ever and failing to hear the speakers. Are you wondering about this omission as well?

The Scriptures tell us the Samaritans believed because of "His own word" (John 4:41). *Word* here is the Greek word, λογον, logon or message. As the Samaritans spend two days with Jesus, they enjoy a first-hand encounter with God's own message to humankind.

Jesus offers us the same chance to spend time with him. He draws us into a conversation with himself. How can that possibly look? Not too long ago, in a great example of how God dotes on us, I witnessed a moment of adoration while at lunch with our small granddaughter. Across the table, my husband asked our favorite two-year-old if she would like to come sit in his lap while we waited for lunch. "No, thank you," she answered. I glanced at him to see if his feelings were hurt.

Instantly, David stretched his hands across the table and gently held her cheeks to secure her attention. "Dear, I love to hear your thoughts," he answered with a chuckle. Isn't that just how God hears all our prayers, even the prayers that were not his first choice for us? Like a grandfather with his beautiful grandchild, Jesus dotes on us in a relationship he values over everything else, even his own life. That's his message to us. We are his beloved children. Our thoughts matter to him.

Opening a New Conversation

Next, we get more humor from the folks who wrote all this down for us. First, the writers confirm many Samaritans believed because "the word of the woman who testified" (John 4:39). She invited them to go meet Jesus for themselves, which they did.

Why is the way they tell the story funny? The writers knew the Samaritans claimed credit for themselves, but they wanted us to know she deserved credit too. Scripture does not contradict itself. The ones telling this story are winking at us. They want us to appreciate the humor of human foibles.

Next, the writers tell us how many Samaritans told a whole different version of the story. Some Samaritans even made a point of telling the woman, "Now we believe, not because of what you said" (John 4:42). I chuckle as I read this account because I can't help but think of neighborhood games in the front yard when I was growing up. *Let's play chase. No, it was my idea, not yours.*

This account really tickles my imagination. Like small children, were her fellow Samaritans taking credit for her good idea to come meet the Savior? It's certainly human nature to want to believe we figured things out by ourselves. It's humorous to think the disciples and Samaritans wanted us to chuckle along with their childish inclination to take credit for themselves. Again, I suspect self-effacing humor made its way into the account to spice it up for us.

However, here's at least one more possible explanation. Were they confirming to her that they too recognized what she believed to be true? Indeed, here is the Christ. "Now we believed, not because of what you said," they affirm. They believe because of what they themselves witness along with her. She is right. He is indeed the Christ. "I am He," he claims to her and they all respond with, "we have heard Him and we know that this is indeed the Christ, the Savior of the world" (John 4:42).

Perhaps both ideas are true. For whatever reason, the writers included this intriguing little nuance. I like the idea of humor here. Humor frees us to use our imagination in all its child-like potential, especially when it comes to living by faith. The writers invite us to laugh together and to admire the confirmation of his deity.

I hope you give yourself permission to let go of any self-condemnation. Instead, my sincere prayer is that you find innumerable new, beautiful, creative, and even humorous ways to join with others to influence those you love. In addition, I pray you have the patience of a farmer, as you plant seeds and watch with joyful anticipation for the harvest.

SEEKING TRUTH AND SECOND CHANCES

There's much we can learn from agriculture, just as Jesus used the harvest for the analogy here. Crops are not grown and harvested overnight. Each one of us is offered a second chance at life by entering a relationship with Jesus. Second chances, just like harvests, often take much longer than we expect. Second chances can take years to implement.

For instance, did you know the pecan tree takes nine or ten years before it reaches full production? Asparagus plants, too, like pecan trees, require patience on the farmer's part, taking two to three years before they produce. "To keep your asparagus bed productive, don't be greedy," Kathy Laliberte writes.[1]

I love her advice, "Don't be greedy." That's wise counsel, whether we're harvesting asparagus or waiting for truth. Pondering takes time. Respecting the time people need to think for themselves is imperative. Fortunately for us, Jesus demonstrated countless strategies for reaching out to people with loving compassion. We've analyzed many in this conversational adventure with the woman at the well, but there are oh-so-many more to be discovered in the Bible.

REJOICING AND TOGETHERNESS: THE RESPONDER'S REWARD

We began looking at this beautiful story to analyze Jesus's proven communication strategies. We desire to be ready and qualified for pure influence in our messy world. We want to draw out deeply authentic conversations with those we love.

Can we put Jesus's communication strategies to work so we have better, more loving companionship throughout our lifetime? Yes. Plus, like the woman at the well, we can inspire fellowship in our families and communities for generations to come. Rejoicing and togetherness is the responder's reward. Most importantly, we want to invite others into an eternal relationship with the Savior.

Will others respond as we try to draw out authentic conversations? We will find out as we go along. One thing's sure, we don't need all the juicy details of past heartbreaks to enter tender conversations with others. We only need compassion and courage.

Like the woman at the well, we do our part when we thoughtfully share what we know to be true. In this, we follow Jesus's own example. How the other person responds is their responsibility, a manifestation of their God-given free will.

Will they reject us? Perhaps. Their objections and baggage may overwhelm their ability to hear, now and forever. Maybe they don't agree and never will. Period.

However, in this one woman's actions, we see how humbly taking responsibility for our own decisions frees others to see

Jesus for themselves. In this story, we have a perfect example of someone who spoke truthfully and humbly, respecting others' right to respond. As they respond to her invitation, joy spreads throughout their community like the warm aroma of apple pies baking at harvest time.

One of my all-time favorite verses says we can love because God loved us first (1 John 4:19). Taking the initiative in conversations may seem scary, but it's proof of our loving attention and commitment to the other person. The woman at the well invited her community to join her in knowing and worshiping God. What a wonderful invitation she offered. No wonder they came quickly when she invited them.

As their conversation unfolded, she stopped being the woman who came to the well alone. Instead, she became a companion of the Savior, and the influential woman who joyfully took a profound message to her community's leaders. Ultimately, the whole community responded and became engaged. In fact, the whole community drew near to Jesus at the well to seek truth for themselves. The result? Joyful companionship with the Savior and with one another.

Jesus talked of harvest. He depicted a lifetime marked by season after season, sowing, reaping, and gathering. He communicated deep understanding of being joyfully one with his Father, working side by side. As Jesus described his love of working side by side with his Father, we notice this woman invited others into conversation with him at the exact same moment. Ah, the joy and reward of togetherness.

AUTHENTIC CONVERSATIONS AND THE REWARD OF COMPANIONSHIP

In this intimate account, we've witnessed a strategic conversational adventure between the woman at the well and her long-awaited Savior. What a beautiful picture of how God patiently seeks us out. He offers us companionship too. In fact, Jesus referred to himself as the bridegroom, a beautiful picture of God's desire for us to enjoy companionship with him for a lifetime and beyond (Matthew 9:35–39). In this way, we know we are loved and wholeheartedly valued by the Savior of the world.

In this story of the woman at the well, we note more than forty principles we can adopt to create better conversations in our own lives. At work or home, in church or in community, these strategies will change lives—especially our own—as we apply them to our own conversations.

We began by looking at the way we all seek relationships that reflect spirit and truth. Jesus overcame human roadblocks to communication and stepped into conversational adventure with an understanding about the sacredness of the human heart. Demonstrating strategic compassion, he prioritized his own rest by withdrawing from those who were unwilling to hear what he had to say. He made himself available to the woman, proving her readiness to hear his message.

Practicing patience, he waited and rested throughout their conversation. He understood her real needs and initially ignored the objections she tossed his way. Jesus sparked her imagination through it all. He chose inclusion, rather than rejection. He used a handy visual aid to describe the over-flowing, cleansing nature of his own Holy Spirit, describing his Spirit as living water.

He honored her ready heart by truthfully acknowledging her past, thus, testing her grit with a factual assessment of her current circumstance. With gentle compassion, he took the sting out of her past by accepting her without rejection.

He made positive assumptions, respecting her intellectual capacity to reason with him. At the perfect time, he addressed her objections with profound understanding. He motivated her with a clear definition of true worship. He sought her companionship as a true worshiper.

Honoring her as a vessel of truth, he helped her recognize her heart's desire. He prepared her to recognize his own true, exceptional identity. Telling the intimate truth, he claimed his true title as Savior. He clearly invited her into his intimate truth, and trusted her, even though she could have chosen to reject him. With humility, he stood against the cultural prejudices of the day.

Trusting her with the next step, Jesus fostered the opportunity for her to influence her whole community. Consequently, the woman adopted several of Jesus's strategies for herself. She shared her own sacred story truthfully and asked an excellent question as she invited others to know the Savior too.

Did the woman at the well get the credit she deserved? That's a debatable point, I guess, but several things seem like credit in the most wonderful way. Jesus endorsed the message she delivered by staying two more days to spend time with the leaders and all whom the woman brought to him. By spending time with them all, he shared his sacred message with them in the new, larger conversation which she initiated.

Like the woman at the well, we may not always get the credit we deserve from the people closest to us. But as surely as the harvest will eventually come, we inevitably cultivate joy and community by sharing authentically. The risk is worth the reward. Just look at how the woman's influence manifested itself. Due to her invitation, the community leaders recognized Jesus and bestowed on him a powerful title.

SAVIOR OF THE WORLD

In Hollywood, titles get cheesier, it seems, with each new movie about a fabled comic book character. In contrast, one unique title resonates throughout history, its power astonishing us even now. *Savior of the World.* Possibly nowhere in Scripture do four little words convey so much joy and revelation. Creator of the Universe. Lord of My Life. Immanuel, God with Us. His titles, like his power, are endless.

Yet, Jesus came to the well and rested. Thirsty and Weary Traveler? Stranger at the Well? Seeking a Lone Samaritan? Man with His Disciples? Giver of Living Water? Such simplicity and power together in one person. All the while, heaven's witnesses behold with bated breath as the drama unfolds. The human mind cannot fathom the rejoicing in heaven as angels witness a whole community influenced by one woman's courageous and humble testimony.

If we want to impact whole communities like the woman at the well, we simply must claim the influence God offers. We can start with the people we know and love most in our own families where gentle companionship can be most cherished.

After our own families, how in the world and big universe can we resist the desire to tell his sacred story to more people? For heaven's sake, why stop with just our own community? Why not stake a claim together on our culture at large too? I urge you to join us in praying and communicating to that end. Amen!

Most importantly for the culture we live in now, there is hope for whole communities to be transformed. My prayer for you is that you are heard whenever you gather the courage to speak strategically and truthfully. May you draw out deeply authentic conversations with those you love. May you influence our messy world for pure good.

Did Jesus include himself when he mentioned the sower, the gatherer, or the reaper, each with different roles and timing? Was he somehow acknowledging the woman at the well as his teammate? Perhaps he included his disciples and the prophets of old. Maybe he even looked to the future and saw you and me. I like to think, resting at the well, his heart warmed at the thought of us entering into his labors and his love now, centuries later.

BEST QUESTION ABOUT TRUTH SEEKING

If I take the risk and share truth will I get the credit I deserve?

I confess, I like it when people give me credit for my hard work or good ideas. Appreciation and gratitude are contagious. Of course, many of my friends are too modest to take any credit at all even when they do terrific stuff. Most of us don't need fame or fortune. But when we work together with a whole team, we especially like for the team to get credit where credit is due. Certainly, we all enjoy the appreciation of those we love most.

When we let down our guard and share our most sacred stories, we hope to be appreciated. Sharing truth always involves the risk of rejection. Perhaps others won't give us the credit we deserve for our bravery and authenticity. But God loves us like a tender bridegroom, seeking us out and never rejecting us.

THE WELL

We can bravely share our most intimate stories with trustworthy fellow-travelers in life. We can face down rejection. When we let down our guard with courage, we commit to loving others in spirit and truth.

As Christians, we rejoice because we have a direct encounter—a real relationship—with the Savior. We enjoy the fellowship and shared purpose Jesus provides for us.

We also enjoy unique freedom as Christians. We can put aside our own baggage to claim our credibility, even when we get no credit at all from anyone but Jesus. We can cherish those around us because we are not distracted by objections and focused on real needs. We freely love others because he loved us first and sought us out. As truth seekers, we invite others to join us in companionship with Jesus and each other. The credibility we claim is Jesus as the Savior, nothing more and no one else.

PRACTICAL TIP: FIND COMMUNITY

Do you feel shy about joining a new group? Has rejection made you afraid to initiate new friendships? Maybe you're a natural introvert. Think about the ways in your life God extends an invitation to you to enjoy community. There are so many places where you may find trustworthy companionship.

A neighborhood coffee shop. A nearby chapel. Your favorite market. A hospital waiting room. A club of volunteers. A phone call or face time. A personal note sent to an acquaintance. Today, why not offer gentle companionship in the moment to someone new and see what happens next?

Perhaps, there's a one-on-one outreach needing volunteers in your community. If you don't feel like you belong to a community at church, consider visiting a different Sunday school class or joining the choir.

Like me, you may spend many happy hours alone at your desk. However, there is no joy like pursuing truth together with those we love. There's accountability in varying perspectives, not to mention fresh insight. We all get a boost of energy when we find those who are willing to share the sacred together in true companionship.

Whatever else you do, take the risk to plug in with trustworthy people. Your beautiful heart and life are worth sharing with others. Above all else, you deserve to be heard and cherished. God wants you to find joy in fellowship and companionship. You were made to be a person of pure, loving influence in our messy world. You have what it takes to draw others into deeply authentic conversations.

MAY WE PRAY TOGETHER?

Dear Father in heaven, we are your children, the ones you love. Help us see each other with a clean slate. Let us welcome others to share their true hearts. Teach us how to invite others into the sacred place where you dwell. You intend for us to exercise the influence you give us. You seek us out and join us. Your credibility becomes ours. We exalt and rejoice in your companionship, O Lord of our hearts. What fortunate people we are to know you. You are the master storyteller, the master communicator.

Who would you like for us to talk to today? What conversational adventures do you have in store for us? Please strengthen us with courage to live your plans for our companionship first thing each and every day. Give us courage to draw deeply from our own hearts to share authentically. Teach us to rejoice together with you, cherishing those you bring across our paths. Bless us now because that's your heart's desire. In Jesus's name. Amen.

"Truth is powerful and it prevails." —Sojourner Truth

ABOUT THE AUTHOR

Cathy Primer Krafve, a native Texan, spent her childhood climbing trees, swimming in the lake, and playing sandlot kickball with her beloved siblings and lots of neighborhood chums.

She's been married to David Krafve for almost forty years, and they have three grown children, two delightful sons-in-law, and seven grandchildren (so far).

Queen of Fun and Coffee Cup Philosopher, Cathy puts a snappy spin on deeply spiritual truths. She draws out deep conversations, based on years of studying the communication techniques Jesus used to convey his message. With experience as a blogger and podcaster (with more than 100,000 monthly listeners), her listening and reading friends learn to leverage compassion and courage in order to engage in two-way conversational adventures.

Her family, affectionately known as Camp *Krafve (CathyKrafve.com)*, is devoted to transmitting healthy, joy-affirming ideas they call "Truth with a Texas Twang!" Today, through *Fireside Talk Radio*, they bring together wise people to share stories of courage, compassion, and companionship.

THE WELL

Having learned most stuff the hard way, Cathy writes with a never-met-a-stranger attitude. Like a friend you met for coffee, she passes along practical strategies for creating conversational adventures, resulting in gentle companionship and a big, beautiful view of communication.

CONNECT WITH CATHY

Cathy really loves reading and listening friends to get in touch. We hope you'll join the Fireside Tribe to receive the free weekly blog about communication and gentle companionship. Please also look for the fun, free tools on her website at CathyKrafve.com.

ENDNOTES

Chapter 1

1 Kerry Patterson, Joseph Grenny, Ron McMillan, Al Switler, *Crucial Conversations: Tools for Talking When Stakes Are High* (New York: McGraw Hill, 2012), 9.

2 John C. Maxwell, *Everyone Communicates, Few Connect: What the Most Effective People Do Differently* (Nashville: Thomas Nelson, 2010), 50.

Chapter 2

1 Restoration Academy, Mission Statement, accessed June 20, 2020, https://www.restorationacademy.org/mission-statement.

2 Matthew McKay, Martha Davis, Patrick Fanning, *Messages: The Communications Skills Book* (Oakland, California: New Harbinger Publications, 2009), 155.

3 Michelle Medlock Adams, "Sassy Faith: Her Wisdom with Michelle Medlock Adams," December 2, 2019, in *Fireside Talk Radio*, produced by Camp Krafve, podcast, MP3 audio, http://www.podtrac.com/pts/redirect.mp3/http://www.toginet.com/podcasts/firesidetalkradio/FiresideTalkRadio_2019-10-30_2.mp3?type=podpage, 4:34–23:30.

Chapter 3

1 Nancy Kay Grace, *The Grace Impact* (Brewster, Kansas: CrossRiver, 2015), 21.

Chapter 4

1 Fred Smith, "What is in your hand?" thegathering, accessed September 27, 2018, https://thegathering.com/what-is-in-your-hand/.

2 Gilbert Bilezikian, *Community 101, Reclaiming the Local Church as Community of Oneness* (Grand Rapids, Michigan:

Zondervan Publishing House, 1997), 43–44.

Chapter 5

1 Shawn Achor, *Before Happiness: The 5 Hidden Keys to Achieving Success, Spreading Happiness, and Sustaining Positive Change* (Crown Publishing Group, 2013), 95.

2 David O Dykes, *Pastor David's Travel Guide to Heaven* (New Jersey: BookBaby, 2017), 11.

3 John Maxwell, *Everyone Communicates, Few Connect* (Nashville: Thomas Nelson, 2010), 30.

Chapter 6

1 Ernest Kurtz and Katherine Ketcham, *The Spirituality of Imperfection, Storytelling and the Search for Meaning* (New York: Bantam Books, 1992), 116.

2 Liz Curtis Higgs, *It's Good to be Queen* (Colorado: Waterbrook Press, 2015), 131.

3 Paula White, *Deal with It: You Cannot Conquer What You Will Not Confront* (Nashville: Nelson Ignite, 2004), 10.

4 White, *Deal with It*, 26.

Chapter 7

1 George Washington and Ross Bolton, *George Washington's 110 Rules of Civility and Decent Behavior in Company and Conversation: The Original and Modern Translation with Illustrations, Historical Notes, and Pictures of Actual Writings* (Createspace Independent Publishing Platform, 2013), 38.

2 Washington and Bolton, *George Washington's 110 Rules of Civility*, 38.

3 "Old Testament: Proverbs," Enter the Bible, Luther Seminary, accessed January 17, 2019, https://www.enterthe-bible.org/oldtestament.aspx?rid=40.

4 CARE, Christ-centered Abortion Recovery and Education, https://careabortionrecovery.com/.

5 Sandy Bristow, "Safe and Secure. Her Wisdom: The Value of Intuition and Healing in Community with Sandy Bristow," February 28, 2018, in *Fireside Talk Radio*, produced by Camp Krafve, podcast, MP3 audio, http://www.podtrac.com/pts/redirect.mp3/http://www.toginet.com/podcasts/firesidetalkradio/FiresideTalkRadio_2018-01-31_2.

mp3?type=podpage, 19:59–8:04.

Chapter 8

1 From a personal email when I asked for his advice. Used with permission.

2 From a personal email when I asked for his advice. Used with permission.

3 Doug McSwane, "Family and Suicide. His Wisdom: When Mental Illness Strikes Your Family with Doug McSwane" and "Family and Suicide. His Story: A Father's Story of his Son's Suicide with Doug McSwane," in *Fireside Talk Radio*, produced by Camp Krafve, podcast, MP3 audio, http://www.podtrac.com/pts/redirect.mp3/http://www.toginet.com/podcasts/firesidetalkradio/FiresideTalkRadio_2018-03-14_2.mp3?type=podpage and http://www.podtrac.com/pts/redirect.mp3/http://www.toginet.com/podcasts/firesidetalkradio/FiresideTalkRadio_2018-03-14_1.mp3?type=podpage.

4 Dana Goodrum, "The Transparent Christian with Dana Goodrum, Reckless Pursuit, Her Wisdom," January 5, 2019, in *Fireside Talk Radio*, produced by Camp Krafve, podcast, MP3 audio, http://www.podtrac.com/pts/redirect.mp3/http://www.toginet.com/podcasts/firesidetalkradio/FiresideTalkRadio_2018-12-05_2.mp3?type=podpage, 6:20–21:40.

Chapter 9

1 Merrill F. Unger, *The New Unger's Bible Dictionary* (Moody Press, Chicago, 1988), 584.

2 Cynthia Tobias, *A Woman of Strength and Purpose: Directing Your Strong Will to Improve Relationships, Expand Influence, and Honor God*, Kindle Edition (WaterBrook, 2016), 6–7.

Chapter 10

1 Dana Goodrum, *Open with Your Broken: Remove the Power of your Past and Gain Freedom in Christ*, Kindle Edition (Certa Publishing, 2018), 1378–1380.

2 Ben Sciacca, "Racial Unity. His Wisdom: Overcoming Racism with Unity, Ben Sciacca, Author of Meals from Mars," February 7, 2017, in *Fireside Talk Radio*, produced by Camp

Krafve, podcast, MP3 audio, http://www.podtrac.com/pts/redirect.mp3/http://www.toginet.com/podcasts/fireside-talkradio/FiresideTalkRadio_2017-12-06_2.mp3?type=pod-page, 23:35–4:26.

Chapter 11

1 Martin Luther King Jr., interview on *Meet the Press*, NBC, April 17, 1960.

2 Rick Johnson, *Better Dads, Stronger Sons, How Fathers Can Guide Boys to Become Men of Character* (Grand Rapids, Michigan: Revell, 2006), 43.

3 Andrew Sobel and Jerold Panas, *Power Questions: Build Relationships, Win New Business, and Influence Others* (Wiley, 2012), 104.

Chapter 12

1 Kathy LaLiberte, "How to Grow Asparagus," accessed January 25, 2019, https://www.gardeners.com/how-to/growing-asparagus/7343.html.

Made in the USA
Monee, IL
12 August 2023

40909135R00122